For M, J & M

Edition 2

Cover artwork by RST Design www.rstdesign.co.uk

Front cover © shutterstock.com/fasphotographic

Back cover © shutterstock.com/mmaxer

www.facebook.com/pcsurname

www.pcsurname.blogspot.co.uk

I'm Just Like You
author unknown

I have been where you fear to be;
I have seen what you fear to see;
I have done what you fear to do;
All these things I have done for you.

I am the one you lean upon,
The one you cast your scorn upon,
The one you bring your troubles to,
All these things I have been for you.

The one you ask to stand apart,
The one you feel should have no heart,
The one you call the "man in blue";
But I am a person, just like you.

And through the years,
I have come to see
That I am not what you ask of me.
So take this badge, take this gun;
Will you take it? – Will anyone?

And when you watch a person die
And hear a battered baby cry,
Then do you think that you can be
All these things you ask of me?

I Pay Your Wages!

A Beginner's Guide to the Police Service

Contents

1. About This Book

This book is for those intrepid people who have been watching far too much TV and enjoy shows with exciting titles like *Car Chase Wars* and *Crime Busters UK*; or maybe it's for those who, like me, watched the *Die Hard* franchise far too many times as an adolescent (not *Die Hard 4.0*, that was terrible!). If this sounds like you then perhaps you're considering applying to join your local police constabulary – serve the public trust, protect the innocent, uphold the law and all that! If you are then this book is intended to give you a humorous, satirical, possibly mildly sarcastic, hopefully not too cynical, but most importantly honest insight into what you can really expect should you one day pull on the black stab vest of power, lace up the boots of justice, fasten the duty belt of public protection, power up the Airwaves radio of righteousness, and wield the black Bic biro of freedom!

Alternatively you might already be part of the thin blue line that stands between order and complete anarchy in this beautiful, green land we call home. If you are 'Job' and reading this book out of curiosity, you could perhaps be on another never-ending scene guard, or maybe reading on a cell watch because your new best friend has finally afforded you a moment's peace and stopped rambling on at you about the voices in their head and the injustices and unfairness in their life that landed them in your custody. Hopefully you will find parallels with your day-to-day work in what I have to say and this will reaffirm that you're not the only idiot out there doing what we do!

Maybe you have no interest whatsoever in joining the police service but are curious about what really goes on behind the closed doors at the police station and out on the dark, mean streets as it cannot really be like the television would have you believe, can it? Whatever your reason for picking up this publication, I hope you enjoy what you read.

You won't find much of that 'law' stuff in here; if it's legislation you're after get yourself one of those Blackstone's manuals that are about the weight and size of a breeze block. Besides, knowing all the law in the world won't help get you through the application process or see you through those first two years' probation; it will just make you a boring guest at any dinner party you're unlikely to get invited to. In fact, in your first couple of years' service, you'll only need to know a few basic laws and acts that will be covered in training school. Only when some time has passed and the moment has come to take your sergeant's exam or move on to a specialist department will you need to take the time to study the delicacies of dealing with sexual offences, murder scene crime management, advanced senior management brown-nosing and the like.

In reward for the long hours, torturous shift pattern and undoubted stress, you will be doing a job unlike any other and a vocation to be proud of. You'll meet new colleagues who will turn in to the greatest friends, prepared to risk their safety to support you because you would do the same for them; small children will wave their hands as you drive by as if you're a superhero (until they reach their teens when some of them, instead of waving a hand, just wave a single finger at you). You don't get many thanks in this job, but the personal satisfaction that comes from knowing you've helped a genuine victim, or locked away a dangerous criminal, is like no other. At times this is the worst job conceivable; but most of the time it's the best in the world – and that is why we love it.

In order to give some credence to what I say and

convince you that I hopefully have some knowledge about the subject matter of this book, I should probably introduce myself. I do not claim to be the greatest 'Super Cop': I cannot tell you how best to investigate a multi-million pound fraud, as truth be told I probably don't know; I cannot describe advanced police firearms tactics and strategies either as that is not my department. I will however share with you what a modern day, front-line police officer does day in, day out, 365 days a year, on the streets of the UK.

I am a serving police constable in an English police force and have been for a few years now, but still have many more to go before retirement. According to my most recent PDR (professional development record) I am 'competent' in most areas of policing – high praise indeed! I am a 'front-line response officer' which means I get to work all manner of inhumane shifts and be at the beck and call of anyone capable of dialling 999 on their phone. If your house gets burgled, your car gets stolen, or your ex-partner's-new-girlfriend's-mother-in-law 'disses' you on Facebook and you call the 'Feds', I will be knocking at your door come rain or shine. If your application is successful and you make it through your basic training, you too will find yourself doing a similar role for at least the first two years' probation period even if your uncle is a chief superintendent (although you can rest assured you will move on to bigger and better things much quicker if he is, irrespective of your ability and accomplishments). A front-line officer can (and will) be expected to deal with any situation that does not fall into the remit of a specialist police department (which are most), or the fire service, or the ambulance service, or the coastguard, Social Services, the local council, RSPCA, the Girl Guides, the AA/RAC and the Highways Agency. Even if the given situation does fall into the remit of one of the aforementioned agencies you will probably still be asked to attend as well just in case there is some remedial task required at the scene that no one else fancies doing.

I write under the pseudonym of PC Surname as some of what you will read will not necessarily be considered politically correct, does not represent the views of the police forces, and – although every attempt has been made to not compromise police confidentiality, tactics or intelligence – some of the content is not what the police politicians would want in the public domain. This book is about giving an honest, open, true and accurate representation of what police life is *really* like.

Finally, as well as leading you from point of application, through basic training, and on to what you might expect to actually be doing when in the job, you will also find littered throughout this book helpful tips, enlightening facts (after all, you can prove anything with statistics – 78.4% of people know that) as well as examples and summaries of the most important and commonly used 'police powers' which any wannabe street cop should know.

All that you read is based on true events and experiences and only the names, times, people, circumstances and actual events have been changed to protect the innocent, the guilty, and most definitely myself in case I am identified and get in trouble with Professional Standards again.

2. Can I Join Up?

FACT: There were 139,110 police officers in England and Wales as of March 2011 according to official Home Office figures.

The Home Office highlights the following basic guidelines for eligibility to apply to join the police:

- There are no minimum or maximum height requirements (removed after the MacPherson report of 1999).
- There is no formal educational requirement, but you will have to pass written tests.
- You must be either a British citizen, a citizen of the EU or other states in the EEA, or a Commonwealth citizen or foreign national with indefinite leave to remain in the UK.
- Although you may still be eligible to join the police service if you have minor convictions/cautions, there are certain offences and conditions that will make you ineligible.
- You must physically and mentally be able to undertake police duties.

Being a police officer is one of the few professional jobs available that actually requires no formal qualifications whatsoever to apply and still commands a reasonable basic starting salary in the low to mid £20k's (depending on geography and how close your force is to London); and you are guaranteed to get a pay rise every year for the first ten years, even if you're rubbish at your job! (See table below for a police constable's pay scale.) The only academic skills you must prove you possess are reasonable numeracy and literacy (although having read some statements from colleagues even this is a 'preferred' rather than 'essential' skill).

Police Constable Pay Scale as of April 2012 from the Home Office

On commencement	£ 23,529
1 Year Service	£ 25,962
2 Years	£ 27,471
3 Years	£ 29,148
4 Years	£ 30,066
5 Years	£ 31,032
6 Years	£ 31,917
7 Years	£ 32,703
8 Years	£ 33,753
9 Years	£ 35,796
10 Years	£ 36,519

Police working in certain areas close to or in London will also receive an additional cost-of-living allowance. It might also interest you to know sergeants can earn up to £45k a year and inspectors £55K.

The Recruitment Process

FACT: 70% of applicants falter at the first hurdle and are rejected at the application form stage. Less than

10% of all applicants are successful and go on to join the police service.

The basic recruitment process is as follows:

Step 1 – The Application Form

The police application form is a long one and has been strategically designed and tested to ensure that – irrespective of age, academic background, gender, race, employment history, or ethnic origin – every applicant is afforded the same chance to be sifted to the next stage of the process.

As well as providing your personal details, qualifications and past employment history, the form will require you to write short accounts of instances in the past when you have portrayed the skills – or 'competencies' – required to one day be a police officer. There is limited space available to demonstrate your talents and continuation pages are not allowed. Candidates should bear in mind that already their literacy is being examined so take your time as poor handwriting, grammar and/or spelling could be costly and halt your application at the first hurdle.

Some forces conduct a final interview before applicants are given start dates and the content of your original application may be referred to. For this reason, I suggest you don't give an example of your skills and abilities based on the summer you spent as an unpaid aid worker in an orphanage in Africa, teaching blind children to see again, whilst spreading a message of democracy and equality unless it's totally true!

TOP TIP: The text in your application form must be authentic and in your words – honesty and integrity is paramount remember – but there is no harm in asking a well-educated friend or family member to check for glaring spelling, grammar or punctuation errors; or perhaps asking a friendly serving police officer (if you have one handy) to peruse the form and offer constructive suggestions prior to you submitting it.

On receiving your form back, the force that you have applied to will check your eligibility and mark your responses to competency questions. The competency areas are as follows:

- Effective Communications – *examples of when you have communicated ideas or information effectively to another person or group of people.*
- Personal Responsibility – *examples of when you have persevered or have had to put in extra effort in order to complete a task.*
- Resilience – *examples of when you have found yourself in a difficult or challenging situation.*
- Race and Diversity – *examples of when you have been required to demonstrate sensitivity or have shown understanding of the needs/views of another person or group of people.*

Getting the application form right is vitally important. Police forces on average receive seven application forms for every single vacancy, and if rejected applicants have to wait six months before they can reapply. *You can find the official NPIA sample application form at the 'I Pay Your Wages' Facebook site along with other useful information – www.facebook.com/pcsurname.*

Here are some Dos and Don'ts to help you along the way:

Do...

- Follow the instructions at the back of the form.
- Complete the form in your own handwriting, using a *black pen*.
- Keep the form clean and tidy; do not cross out or spill your tea on it.
- Make photocopies of the form and practise filling it out before completing the final version.
- In the competency examples the assessors want to know what *you* did. Use phrases like "I did this because", "I identified", "I decided".
- Consider typing your competency answers using a word processor first to check for any spelling/grammar errors.

Don't...

- Do not use examples of when you were a child in the competency section.
- Use phrases like "we did this".
- Write outside the space provided – it will not be marked.
- Leave any of the form blank – you will be doomed to failure
- Give generalised competency examples. They must be specific to the competencies being examined.
- Do not lie on your application form! You will be found out!

If your application is successful, you will be invited to attend an assessment centre.

Step 2 – The Assessment Centre

At an assessment centre you will again demonstrate your numeracy and literacy in a short exam and twenty-minute structured interview, before your problem-solving skills are put to the test in dynamic role plays based around the same competencies and skills mentioned in step 1, as well as three new areas:

- Race and Diversity
- Community and Customer Focus
- Problem Solving
- Effective Communication
- Resilience
- Team Working
- Personal Responsibility

The role-plays are set around a non-police-related setting – currently a fictitious shopping centre. Candidates will be asked to assume roles based around the shopping centre; for example a customer service adviser, or human resources officer. Basically, you will be given a brief of the scenario that awaits you and, having only a few minutes to prepare, you will be presented with a room full of one or possibly several 'actors' who you will have to engage with and appease. Sitting quietly in a corner will be an assessor hopefully ticking off boxes as you go. The actors themselves are given short scripts and responses which they cannot deviate from so in truth are more like robots than BAFTA-winning thespians – although still less wooden than those you see on *Hollyoaks*! The scenarios are usually based around small dilemmas and the candidate must extract the relevant information, show understanding towards the causes and the impact on the afflicted, before ideally suggesting a solution or compromise.

The itinerary of the assessment centre day will be as follows (in no particular order):

- A competency-based interview with 4 questions lasting 20 minutes in total.
- A numerical reasoning test lasting 12 minutes.
- A verbal logical reasoning test lasting 25 minutes.
- Two written exercises lasting 20 minutes each.
- Four interactive exercises lasting 5 minutes each (role plays).
- All candidates undertake the same exercises and are assessed on an equal basis. The assessment lasts approximately half a day.

TOP TIPS FOR PASSING THE ASSESSMENT:

- *If you have time in the numerical and written exercises, take the chance to read through your answers, check and double-check. Do not rest on your laurels.*
- *On the maths and verbal reasoning – if you can't answer a question still give an answer. It's multiple choice so a 1 in 4 chance of getting it right is better than nothing.*
- *Again on the multiple choice papers, if you miss a question out intending to come back to it, then make a note of it.*
- *Make sure you read through the information pack that you are sent, but don't panic about not remembering everything. You just need an understanding of it.*
- *If you are unsure of what you are being asked to do, then don't be afraid to ask an invigilator. Chances are you're not the only one.*
- *It's no coincidence that the assessment centre is hard to prepare for; the idea is to place would-be-officers under pressure, out of their comfort zones and test their mettle. However, if it's been a few years since school, it might be worth brushing up on basic*

spelling and mental arithmetic to give yourself the best opportunity with the exam part of the day.
- Take time to read everything through carefully, so that you don't misinterpret anything.
- For the interview think carefully about what example you are going to use beforehand so you can go straight into your talk.
- In everything you do remain diverse. Don't take sides with anyone but instead look at the situation from the perspective of everyone involved.
- Remember you are being assessed at all times, even when not actually 'being assessed', so be mindful of what you say and how you react.

Step 3 – Final Clearance

Next, after successfully negotiating the pit-falls of the assessment, your references will be contacted and you'll undergo background, security, medical and eyesight checks. Immediate family members will also be security checked. This is also where you do your fitness test and be fitted for uniform.

At this stage some forces may choose to run additional assessments, such as the final interview mentioned in Step 1.

Skills to Pay the Bills?

So, to be a police officer you must have mastered the English language and demonstrate you can calmly communicate with folks from all walks of life without being racist, prejudiced or discriminatory. Your suitability to be a police officer will be assessed by how you fill out a detailed application form, how you perform in dynamic role plays at an assessment centre, and finally by whether or not you're patient enough to wait up to several years to be invited for a medical and physical with your desired force prior to employment commencing. The latter depends on the police force's recruitment policy at the time of application. To speed you along this path, when filling out your application form you may wish to consider changing your gender, race, ethnicity, sexual orientation, religion and/or disabilities – so choose wisely when ticking those boxes. If you're a half-black, half-Chinese, bisexual, Buddhist transgender with mild learning difficulties you can probably start tomorrow! Being serious for just a moment though, the police come in contact with people from all backgrounds and ethnicities; having a diverse makeup of rank-and-file officers populates the police with fresh views and perceptions, which can only be of benefit, as well as making the police service more approachable to all.

Fitness

Another area that gave me great concern all those years ago when I applied were doubts about if I was physically fit enough. When I recall these apprehensions now I almost laugh out loud at my naivety! As long as you can walk at a brisk pace and have enough strength in your arms to carry a full court charge file for a domestic harassment case – photocopied in triplicate – up 5 flights of stairs to the Crown Prosecution Service offices, then you'll be fine passing the fitness test!

Your fitness is assessed by undertaking a bleep test over a 15 metres track, up to a very low level that even an asthmatic, drug-riddled, ADHD-afflicted, malnourished, future 'customer' of yours could even pass. The bleep test is one you might have done at school and candidates are currently only required to attain a very modest level of 5.4. The fitness standards were lowered some years ago so more women could join. Since female officers only run after and then fight female criminals this makes perfect sense (sarcasm alert)! More cynical colleagues would call this 'positive discrimination', but I have long learnt that all forms of discrimination were stamped out of the police service by the Home Office in 1984 with the introduction of the Police and Criminal Evidence Act (PACE).

Fortunately the majority of female officers I know are by far scarier and handier in a scrap than their male counterparts, so excel in their role despite the patronising fitness test. Once in the job, you will be required to demonstrate you can maintain these meagre fitness levels at annual intervals. Don't fret though – should you fall below the standards, rather than be taken off front-line duties you will be given an Action Plan to regain your former athleticism. I assume this action plan will say things like "eat less cake" and "do more exercise", and then you just try again in six weeks.

That's not to say it won't be beneficial to ensure your fitness standards well exceed those required. Crime fighting is a physical job – people will run away and you will have to give chase. You will also get in confrontations with people and will at some stage roll around on the floor with someone – I guarantee it! Some say you're not doing your job right unless people are trying to assault you. Although infrequent, there are dangers in this job and courage and fortitude as well as physical strength are essential – we don't wear stab vests just to look menacing you know! Not until you reach the dizzy heights of Chief Inspector are you assured of the relative safety of a comfy office chair and desk and will you no longer have to interact with aggressive members of the public.

Medical

As well as being examined by a force medical officer, hopefuls are also drug-tested via a urine sample. The examiner is looking for any signs that the potential recruit will not be able to give thirty plus years of loyal service to the crown.

Another stumbling block for potential candidates in the past was pre-existing medical conditions. Whereas before afflictions like asthma, diabetes, dyspraxia, genital warts and the flesh-eating Ebola virus might have blighted an application at the outset, police forces are now equal-opportunity employers. Each applicant must be judged individually in respect of their health and, as a consequence, their ability to do the job for a reasonable period of time. This means that as long as you are physically capable of doing the tasks entailed in modern policing and your health issues should not affect that in the future, then your application will still be considered. If this concerns you it is best to make some very polite enquiries with your prospective police forces' occupational health officers as they might have the ultimate say so.

Eyesight is another potential spanner in the works. Each force will have its own unaided (without glasses or contacts), and aided standards which new recruits must meet. There will be even more stringent eyesight requirements should you one day wish to take specialist training like advance driving or firearms courses. On the plus side, many laser eye specialists will give discounts for emergency service workers. I got mine zapped several years ago and it was some of the best money ever spent: I remember sitting in the chair with my eyes clamped open and being able to smell my own corneas burning as the laser went to work. Mmm! For a week afterwards, the pain was excruciating – like someone was constantly rubbing salt and vinegar crisps into my eyes – and all I could do was sit in a darkened room, afraid to even blink because of the agony, gently sobbing to myself. Hope that hasn't put you off though...

You also have to be aged at least 18 1/2. Most forces prefer applicants to be aged in their mid-20's though, as they should have gained 'life experience' by then, but don't let this put you off if you are a hungry, young whippersnapper. The current police pension requires you to now work 35 years (used to be 30) to get a full pay out and you can only work as a front-line officer until you are 55, so don't delay, apply today!

Background Checks

You must not be in any financial difficulties. Upon application all candidates are credit checked and any significant debts or arrears will halt proceedings. The reason behind this is whilst in the job police officers regularly come into contact with cash and valuables – usually seized from an unsuspecting drug dealer. Why just the other week I found in someone's wardrobe and held in my hand a lump of crumbly white powder that a detective sergeant later told me was worth £200k! A police officer's honesty and integrity must be paramount and the argument is that if you have debt, you might be tempted, and therefore bring the police into disrepute.

Finally, to get in the police, you can't be a criminal. Minor indiscretions like traffic tickets or convictions as a youth might not scupper your chances, but if in your early life you regularly ventured across to the dark side and were arrested then these bad marks will most likely count against you.

However, if you did grow up on the wrong side of the tracks, and your mates were known to dabble in criminal activities, but you didn't get involved – just paid close attention – you will be at a distinct advantage over your fellow fresh faced recruits with only their university degrees in criminology and law (as well as the skills to make the perfect cheese toasty) behind them come day one at training school. If you are concerned about some of the poor decisions you made before becoming the reformed character you are now, speak with your force's recruitment team and they'll advise you accordingly. Background checks will also be carried out on your immediate family so please bear this in mind too.

Do not try to hide anything on your application form – I know I'm repeating myself but I cannot stress this enough! Be honest as anything found to be untrue or undisclosed at a later date will result in immediate exclusion – irrespective of how far down the recruitment process you are – or immediate termination of your employment if you have successfully done the hard bit and gotten yourself a job in the police.

TOP TIP: Some universities and colleges now offer specific qualifications in Policing. Although further education should never be discouraged, check carefully as, although this shows dedication and commitment come the applicant's interview, many forces do not recognize these specific qualifications at all or, if they do, this will only become relevant many years down the career path when very high up the police rank pyramid.

Still interested? Then read on.

3. Unofficial Skills

Mentioned in the previous chapter were official criteria that you will have to satisfy to register an application. What follows are unofficial traits that once in the job will be far more beneficial.

Patience

Especially in your first two years, during your 'student officer' or probationary period, you will find yourself undertaking all manner of lengthy activities that will test this skill to the maximum. It's highly likely you'll hit your 'shift' (team) being unable to drive a police vehicle at all, let alone on adrenaline-fuelled, blue-light runs along busy high streets. So every mundane and tiresome job that no one else wants to do will fall on you. This is a rite-of-passage all 'probies' (probationers) must go through. I spent what must have literally totalled days on my own, guarding pools of blood on pavements outside night clubs, or standing outside a flat that had had horrific atrocities occur inside just because scenes of crime officers (SOCO) could not come out until the morning.

This brings me on to another linked specialist skill that will prove invaluable: being able to hold your bladder for incomprehensible periods of time. Mastering advanced bladder control will no doubt render your prostate useless later on in life, but will save you great embarrassment in the short term. I recently attained a respectful Level 3 Bladder Control Status by successfully guarding a muddy allotment where a dog walker had found bones that may or not have been human. It was 6 hours before I was relieved by a colleague and therefore had the opportunity to relieve myself as well. Had it been much longer, any forensic chemical tests of the soil's composition may have resulted in unexpected results as I would have had no alternative. Legend tells of Level 7 'Grand Master' of Bladder Control on C Section at a station over the other side of the constabulary, but I have not met him and can only wonder at the suffering he must have endured during that 15-hour shift. Incidentally, the bones turned out to be the remains of a large ostrich. How the wretched bird remains got there and as a result nearly ruined my trousers is to this day an unexplained mystery which I have no interest in solving!

TOP TIP: If, prior to leaving station for what the radio controller describes as a 'quick enquiry' you have the opportunity to answer a call of nature – take it!

Having patience also comes in the form of being able to listen to a seemingly endless supply of drunk people in front of the same night clubs that the inevitable pool of blood will also appear outside later that very evening (the one that you might find yourself guarding). The club's crafty/greedy owners regularly run drink promotions designed to extract all the benefit money from the punters' pockets with no consideration for the strain this puts on the emergency services, hospitals and council workers whose job it is to clean up dried pools of blood.

There is a lot of waiting around and enforced procrastination in the role of a police officer – waiting for solicitors in custody, waiting for the Crown Prosecution Service to make a charging decision, waiting for arrestable suspects to come out from the rock under which they are hiding. The rickety old wheels of justice do turn but at a very slow rate sometimes. As an eager and enthusiastic young constable it can be very frustrating but keep your chin up and do not allow it to detract from your ultimate goals.

Time Management

The modern police officer takes on many different and diverse roles. As well as a professional law-man/law-woman, you are also expected to be a semi-professional social worker, educator, health care practitioner, night-club steward, traffic controller, taxi driver, accountant and truant officer to name but a few. This list is non-exhaustive as new roles and pressures are forced upon police officers all the time as new policies and hair-brain schemes materialise. It is also nice, but not essential, if you can solve crimes and bring nogoodniks to justice as well whilst you're at it. If you're very lucky, there are only 40 hours a week in which to fulfil all your roles.

At any one time I can have up to a dozen crime reports on my case load. My case load is monitored via a computerised crime management system. As a humble PC the crimes I am the 'officer in charge' (OIC) of tend to be low-level crimes, or higher-level crimes that, at present, have no realistic chance of an 'offender' or 'suspect' (baddy) being arrested and therefore the crime being solved so the detectives in CID aren't interested in taking it off my hands. Incidentally, if it is a higher-level crime and the suspect can easily be arrested and the crime solved then someone in a far more important department that works 8 a.m. until 4 p.m. during the week would have the crime report off me as quick as a flash.

My crime reports usually range from assaults, thefts of all kinds, burglaries, harassments and criminal damages. Not the stuff prime-time dramas on ITV are made of I'm sure you'll agree. I heard that an officer I work with once briefly held a crime report for the offence of Riding A Horse Furiously On a Public Highway contrary to Section 28 of the Town Police Clauses Act of 1847, but that turned out to be a clerical error.

It is my responsibility to use my time wisely to progress my crime reports through good investigation practices to a hopeful conclusion of the baddy being arrested, charged, convicted and sent to prison. Along the way I must keep my victims updated as to my progress. This doesn't sound too tricky, however you must factor in obstacles that will be placed in my way; an example would be night shifts. Victims become very angry and soon make complaints if you eagerly update them at 2 a.m. on a Tuesday morning that their sister-in-law has finally been arrested for stealing Tiger, the victim's Staffordshire bull terrier (I found this out to my cost early on in my service). It's also hard to investigate crime at the same time as searching for missing children, escorting prisoners to hospital for usually fictitious illnesses, dealing with traffic collisions and offering relationship advice to rowing couples.

IT Skills

I can count at least 30 computer systems used by myself and colleagues. Some are used daily and some are used so infrequently that when it does come time to use them, I've forgotten how and have to be retrained. But all have unique password systems used to gain access which expire and have to be manually changed at varying intervals. Of course each computer system's password will have to be different lengths, made up of different characters and might be numerical, alphabetical or have to be a combination of both and previous passwords cannot be repeated. Usually you are allowed three attempts to guess your password before the system locks you out and you must email the IT help desk to get a new one (this is assuming it's not the email system you've locked yourself out of). I assume the 'help' part of 'IT help desk' can only be an attempt at ironic police humour as they are by far the most unhelpful people in the universe. Ejector seat on a helicopter springs to mind.

We also now have Blackberries. This really impresses the youths. I am briefly "down with the kids, you get me?", until I tell them I haven't got the Facebook app, they cannot BBM me, I can't play Angry Birds on it and no – they can't follow me on Twitter. However, as well as checking emails (password permitting) and downloading briefings on the go, I can also run PNC (Police National Computer) checks; assuming I'm not locked out of the PNC system at the time I desire to use it.

As well as holding vehicle and insurance information, the PNC lists details about every individual who is known to the police. Here I can find out previous convictions, bail conditions, addresses, descriptions and warning markers about anyone standing in front of me and who will give me their name and date of birth. The warning markers are particularly handy if it's an angry-looking, knuckle-dragging, tattooed, lumbering hulk of a man in front of me who I might have to be singlehandedly arresting shortly. These markers take many forms. For example, if a criminal has not even got at least a 'VIOLENT' marker to their name, they'll almost certainly get laughed out of their social housing estate! Most markers are self-explanatory like DRUGS, WEAPONS, FIREARMS, CONTAGIOUS, ESCAPER and FEMALE IMPERSONATER (seriously). Regular offenders gradually accrue markers over their criminal careers. Once they've attained their 4th warning marker, they get the 5th free under the PNC loyalty scheme! (Not really.)

Common Sense

I'm going say something controversial now. Something that goes completely against the Home Office, my training, and the views of my high ranking superior officers who sit in air-conditioned offices at HQ. Something so radical and revolutionary I leave myself open to immediate expulsion from the police and potentially society as a whole if this is traced back to me:

A common sense approach is a good thing!

There, I've said it.

The police have been campaigning for years to have discretion back and reduce police bureaucracy. Every government promises to 'cut red tape' and 'put bobbies back on the streets', but we're yet to see much fruition. The police would love to deliver an effective service and sort out 'Broken Britain', but we can't because we are handicapped by political correctness, health and safety and a limp-wristed administration. Until someone gets to grip with this, little will change and the police will continue to be responsible for all the world's problems in the eyes of some narrow-minded members of the public who are coerced by the media:

Soaring crime rates across the country? Police's fault – not patrolling in their cars enough. The great big hole in the ozone layer? Police's fault – patrolling in their cars too much. The financial crisis crippling the world's economy? Also police's fault – spending too much money on patrol cars and then using them too much or not enough.

We're slowly moving in the right direction but there's still a long way to go. We're still forced to criminalise 12-year-olds for pinching Mars bars from the Co-op or, perhaps worst still, instead arresting for assault the father of the 12-year-old for clipping his troubled offspring around the ear for pinching confectionary from the Co-op.

Rant over.

Some police officers have masters degrees and the IQ of Stephen Hawkins to go with it, but still couldn't find the perpetrator even if he was stood over the bloody corpse, with a knife in his hand, shouting "I done it!". Common sense is just as valuable a commodity as any qualification and sets apart the competent but unexceptional from those that will aspire to greater things and make a real difference combating crime in a proactive, specialist unit one day.

The Ability to Function Without Sustenance and Sleep

If you are reading this book, it is a fair assumption that you are most likely human. However, for many years now the role of the front-line police officer has been evolving and is now no longer suited to your average, humanoid, carbon based life form. The primary disadvantage of the humanoid species with regard to being agents of modern law enforcement is that humans constantly need to feed and water themselves, whilst also requiring by law a minimum of 11 hours between shifts, thus diminishing their efficiency to uphold the laws of the land.

If you have perfected the ability to go without these inconvenient human flaws – perhaps you are an extra-terrestrial silicon-based being – then you will be able to carry out your role with unequivocal proficiency. And you will tick a diversity box on the application form too!

Police Officer's Nose

This is a talent which a young in-service officer must quickly develop to survive in the urban jungle. A type of sixth sense for when something is amiss, perhaps not as it firsts seems, or someone is not telling the full story.

Like a stab vest-clad Jedi, an astute officer will arrive at a job, quickly establish what has happened and identify who is to be arrested. Some say that the ability to spot the correct baddy – or 'scroat' to use unofficial police terminology – at the scene of an incident is a natural, God-given talent that only the lucky few command and, like the goal-scoring talent Wayne Rooney possesses, cannot be taught.

Speaking of the mercurial, Scouse goal machine brings us on nicely to the appearance of the average scroat on the street, as spotting said scroat (and therefore likely offender) is all part of this trick:

I must stress 'Scroatness' has nothing to do with class, background, economics or education; it is about how people *choose* to behave as their moral compass is somewhat out. Everyone has seen a scroat. They are the people that freely swear and spit in public in the presence of your children, the type that litters your streets without hesitation as someone else will clean up after them, and those who park in disabled spaces without consideration as to find a proper space would be far too much effort etc.

The male scroat will be unemployed because he can't be *'bovvered'* to get a job and lives on a housing estate. His council tax, unlike mine and probably yours, will be paid for him by the government so I am not fooled when he tells me "I pay your wages!" He will spend his days drinking cheap lager, smoking cannabis, watching his huge flat-screen TV and/or eating junk food. A modern 21st century scroat is very particular about his attire as this is one way he expresses his individual character and personality. Often preferring to clothe himself like a reject from an N-Dubz tribute group, the common scroat can be observed hanging around shopping centres or McDonalds car parks.

The female scroat, the fairer of the scroat sex, is also unemployed and spends her days watching (or appearing as a guest on) Jeremy Kyle and/or Trisha. Her primary role is the manufacture of children, or 'scroatlings', which she can produce at an alarming rate. (She will then inevitably give her brood imaginative and exotic names.) As well as wearing the obligatory tracksuit and/or hoody, the female scroat is also noticeable by the copious amounts of make-up beautifying her face, and the large golden hooped earrings that complete her look. Often hunting in packs, the scroatettes can be seen pushing buggies along the high street usually in the direction of Aldi. Both male and female variants have very poor dental hygiene.

The traditional scroat courtship custom is one of the most wonderful, beautiful and natural phenomena one can behold. The female will signal to the males that it is her intention to take a mate by decorating herself in the shortest, smallest and most revealing clothing that Primark can provide, ensuring as much tattooed flesh is on view as possible. Her hair will be scraped back from her forehead and tied in the ceremonial pony tail. The female's skin will have taken on an orange glow and her face will be adorned in foundation several millimetres thick. Clutching a clearly counterfeit designer handbag, she is finally ready to find her prince so will make her way to the mating ground – in this case namely Lava & Lights (AKA Lager & Fights) Nite Club on the high street. There she will meet the single males. Keen to impress, he will be wearing his best tracksuit bottoms (the same ones he wears to important court cases). The tracksuit bottoms will have no cords in them as he has also worn them when making regular stays at the free hotel with the blue plastic mattresses and free and independent legal advice (anything that could be used as a ligature is always removed from prisoners in custody). The lack of a cord has nothing to do with him wearing his trousers just under his backside either. The single males will compete for her attention by beating their chests – as well as other drunken rivals faces – until the dominant alpha scroat is established.

His and her eyes will meet and the magic will start to happen. The two will converse with each other in a dialect known as 'Scroatish'; a very similar language to English only with more profanity, less syllables and vocabulary that is as bad as, like, whatever, innit:

Wayne: "You are like so fit, ****, I swear down you could be in them Saturdays".
Sharon (smiling and blushing): "Shut up! That is a well nice thing to say, ****."
Wayne: "I think I seen you in the Job Centre de other day."
Sharon: "Yeah, ****, dey tried to stop my child benefit! I was not happy, innit!"

Wayne: "Yeah, I know. Dem tried to mug me off like that just coz I've not had a job for 3 years! Dey tried to get me to work at the car wash, but I was like – whatever, I ain't ****ing Kosovian!"

Sharon: "Dat is so ****ing unfair. What da ****! You got any weed on ya?"

Wayne: "Yeah, you want some ...?"

Over several pints of Stella and many bottles of unbranded Bacardi-based alcopops, the happy couple will fall in love and discuss getting matching tattoos. Wayne may even buy Sharon a doner kebab if trying really hard to woo her. Finally the relationship will be consummated in the back of a Citroën Saxo.

Naturally, the relationship will come to a crashing and violent end when Wayne sleeps with Sharon's best friend Tulisa. Next will come the obligatory name calling on Facebook, threats, late night drunken banging on each other's doors, and accusations and counter accusations that one is harassing the other (guess who gets to sort that out?!). All of the hostilities will however have come after Wayne has impregnated Sharon. After a nine-month gestation period, Sharon will give birth to a bouncy Wayne Jnr., brother to her other two children Beyonce and Kane. The circle of life goes on and the gene pool is diluted just a little bit more. Magical in a way ...

4. Reasons to Become a Police Officer

FACT: There are 43 regional police forces in England and Wales as well as 8 in Scotland; not to mention British Transport Police and the Civil Nuclear Constabulary who are based all over the country.

As if the allure of wearing a sexy black uniform and spending your time chasing after miscreants isn't enough, before you submit an application you must also question your own motives for wanting to be part of the thin blue line. Are you applying for the right reasons? Here are some of the *real* reasons people join the police service.

Because I Watch Too Much TV

Although they'd never admit it, this is the real reason most people attempt the 25-page police application form. Being a cop is cool, right? Only the most foolhardy still believe *The Bill* was an accurate portrayal of modern policing – there is far more drama and sexual scandal in real life! But even the plethora of fly-on-the-wall style documentaries do not often accurately reflect the day-to-day work of the police though. Have you ever heard Jamie Theakston say, "On this week's episode we join PC Johnson of the Roads Policing Team as he completes an urgent file upgrade because – although the CPS have known about the impending court case for many weeks – they have only just sent an email requesting the full file urgently"? Don't forget, literally days of footage is shot to condense down enough action to make just eight 1-hour-long episodes for the police-obsessed general public to devour.

Incidentally, being in the police ruins any enjoyment that you (and especially the people sitting with you) might have had before when watching fictional cop shows on either the big or small screen. You will constantly find yourself saying out loud things like "His superiors would never let him get away with that, so unrealistic" or "He's got no grounds to kick that door in and enter" and "That is a flagrant breach of PACE!"

Being a police officer is at times very exciting and you will get to chase after evildoers, drive cars fast, fight drunken people and maybe even save some lives. But it is not a job to be taken lightly and not a job you 'might give a try'. Once you have strip searched and intimately examined a crack and heroin addict, and found concealed packages of the drugs in the most unthinkable of orifices, you will soon realize the job of a front-line police officer is not a glamorous one. Although comparably well paid to some other public service jobs, unless an individual truly wants to be a police officer and is prepared to work hard and make sacrifices, perhaps some applicants should look elsewhere. Is the fire service recruiting maybe?

Because the Fire Service Wouldn't Have Me

The police and 'Trumpton' have a funny relationship. Although ultimately we have to get on with them and both are professional, there is still a bit of animosity bubbling under the service. No one can really say why, but I guess it comes down to professional rivalry and who is the best emergency service (sorry ambulance service, you do an amazing job under the circumstances, but this is a two-horse race). There is little doubt who are the best physically as the fire service win hands down there. They also seem far better funded and equipped as their toys far exceed ours: in their trucks they have breathing apparatus, high tech cutting equipment (hacking the roofs off crashed cars is by far their favourite pastime), inflatable river rescue tools, laser-synched flashing lights and the shiniest helmets you'll ever see, to name but a few. In the back of my panda (medium sized patrol car, named after the traditional black and white livery once worn by them) I'm lucky to have three orange cones, an empty first aid kit and a broom to sweep up RTC (Road Traffic Collision) debris! I heard from an ex-fire fighter who had since seen sense and joined the winning team that the 'splash-and-dash' boys' opinion of the 'boys in blue' deteriorated further when the fire service went on strike in 2002 over their pay and conditions. If you recall the army were drafted in with their antique 'Green Goddesses' to ensure some sort of contingency was in place. As the police supported the army and not the fire fighters on the picket line, they have had a bee in their bonnets ever since. I'm not sure how true this is, but one thing *is* for sure: if you want to impress the opposite sex, join the fire service! They're the real heroes after all! Plus they get to sleep during their night shifts instead of going out 'patrolling' for fires and cats in trees.

Although it pains me to admit it, the fire service does a magnificent job (as do the paramedics) in the same difficult financial, social and litigious modern world we now live in.

Because I Was Bullied at School

Members of the public ask me about this fairly often. Strangely, it inevitably comes immediately prior to or after someone gets arrested. Let me give you an example of such an occurrence that happens up and down night spots all over the country on Friday and Saturday nights:

Yob: *"...but why have I gotta leave, I ain't done nothin' wrong!"*
PC Surname: *"The door staff have asked you to leave, now move it."*
Yob: *"This is b******s! I ain't moving."*
PC Surname: *"You're in public, if you swear again you're liable to get arrested."*
Yob: *"**** off!"*
PC Surname: *"Right, that's it! You're nicked ..."*
Yob: *"I'd bang you out if you weren't in that uniform! I bet you got bullied at school or summin'!"*
PC Surname: (on the police radio) *"Can we have the van outside Lava and Lights please!"*

Being a police officer and the uniform that comes with it means you can do and say a lot more than you would normally get away with as a civilian. But this is a privilege not to be abused. It has been said before that in this country the populous are policed by consent. This means that despite the low public opinion of the police, which is created by a fickle media to sell papers, the average person on the street will still do as told when it is done respectfully by the man/woman in blue. That's not to say that there aren't a few jumped up little Hitlers that I know of in my force, but fortunately these are few and far between. New recruits quickly learn it is how and not what you say to someone that will be the difference between having a compliant prisoner, or instead having a prisoner spitting and shouting at you as you roll around on the floor with him, desperately trying to summon assistance on your radio.

Because My Home Life is Too Settled and I Spend Too Much Time With My Family and Friends

Then the police force is perfect for you! Apply today! Life in the police is almost guaranteed to put strain on even the strongest relationship. Many a marriage has been obliterated within six months of an officer starting shift work. Unfortunately, due to the uniqueness of the work and stresses that come with it, often partners who are not in the job find it hard to understand why their once sensible, loving and caring, dedicated sweetheart comes home at the end of a shift a frazzled, cynical, neurotic, imbalanced tool of law enforcement. This is probably also a contributory factor as to why so many officers are unfaithful. Every police station is awash with rumours of who is sleeping with whom behind whose back. Sad, but true. It is easy to get engrossed in an exciting new career and neglect those closest, so factor into your thinking how shift work will affect your work-life balance before it's too late.

FACT: It has been well documented that one in every two marriages in this country ultimately ends in divorce. All research shows police relationships suffer a substantially higher divorce rate with estimates of between 60-75%. Reassuring reading for any newlyweds!

Because I Want to Find a Husband/Wife

Another fantastic reason to sign up! Even the most pug-ugly probationary officer is bound to find love in the police service. Remember, not only are there hundreds of recently separated men and women on the rebound as a result of the relationship strain (see above), but there are also a whole host of PCSOs and civilian staff to whet the appetite too! Don't expect to keep any new blossoming relationship out of the hottest station gossip and rumour mill though; by definition police officers are naturally inquisitive people and rumours – regardless of their accuracy – spread like wildfire around stations as I mentioned before. Be warned though, even the most successful officers have ruined good careers and lost pensions by being in the intimate company of someone they should not have. An old sweat, now retired, once warned me the 'Four P's' will get you the sack in this job: 1. Paperwork, 2. Property (of the seized/found variety), 3. Pocket Note Books (PNB) and 4. Policewomen (or men)! So keep your paperwork in order, your property safe, your pocket note book up to date, and your penis in your pants! (Or the female equivalent if you have no penis... erm ...you know what I mean!)

Because I Want To Be All I Can Be

A noble cause indeed. Other than using police employment as a form of speed dating as mentioned above, recruits of all ages will develop new skills that not only assist them in furthering their career, but that will also benefit them in all walks of their lives in and out of uniform. Police officers are exposed to an overabundance of situations that mere civilians could not possibly comprehend and as such develop new levels of confidence, resilience and understanding. Although at times very challenging, 'no two days are alike' (if you'll pardon the cliché) and because of this, officers have the privilege and burden of witnessing at close quarters the most extraordinary things.

As well as expanding their personal skill sets,

officers will also have the chance to go places off limits to the public, be privy to information concealed from the public domain, experience unique scenarios, as well as meeting interesting characters from all backgrounds.

Because my Father, Mother, Uncle, Aunt, Brother, Sister, etc. was a Copper

There are many second- or even third-generation officers that I can name in my humble force. Following in relatives' footsteps is quite common. But having roots in the police by no means guarantees success. The officer who makes a name for themselves with hard work and the right attitude, rather than off the back of their relation's reputation, are the ones respected the most.

I often feel sorry for new recruits as I see them struggle to emulate their parent(s) or family in the job they've been groomed for their whole life. Sometimes it is evident to all but the young officer themselves that they are just not cut out for the job. But, like a young Anakin Skywalker, they feel compelled to persist as failure is not an option and they must fulfil their destiny (my second *Star Wars* reference). Just because The Force is strong in you and your midi-chlorian count is off the scale doesn't mean this is the right job for you. After all, just look what happened to young Anakin – he became the chief superintendent... I mean Lord Darth Vader! (Apologies to those not fans of the franchise.)

Although senior officers would strenuously deny it, especially when it comes to promotion, it can be a case of *who* and not *what* you know that can mean the difference between success and failure. Police politics is a valuable weapon to wield.

Because of the Career Opportunities

Ooh, that's a good one! Another plus with police employment is the meandering path your 35+ year career can take. There are dozens of specialist departments to consider once you've learned about grass roots policing in your tentative first years in the job. Some are more exciting than others:

If you have a penchant for wearing sunglasses at work, your neck is thick, you have a superiority complex over lesser officers, you have a gym membership and enjoy protein shakes, as well as a fondness for leaving chaos and paperwork in your wake for someone else to clear up at every incident you attend, maybe you can master the ancient art of bang-gang stick and lightning caster (AKA firearm and taser) and join the Firearm Support Unit!

Although sometimes enviously mocked by their divisional peers for being macho glory hunters, firearms officer wannabes have to demonstrate much higher fitness standards than normal frontline personnel, as well as exceptional shooting accuracy and weapons craft before undertaking an intense and long training course. Only the best are then handpicked for the role. Their fitness and skills are then constantly monitored to ensure standards do not slip.

FACT: If as a last resort a firearms officer is required to discharge their weapon at a subject they do so with the intention of instantly removing that threat. In all likeliness this will result in a mortal wound to the subject. Officers are then trained to administer immediate life-saving medical assistance to the subject. After firing the officer will be suspended from duty for several months pending an independent inquiry into their decision making and subsequent actions.

Alternatively if fast cars and chases are your thing, the traffic department might await you. Using the specialist crime fighting vehicles at their disposal, these guys and gals hurtle around at breakneck speed scouring the roads for people not wearing seat belts, talking on their phones and using their front fog lights despite visibility being greater than 100 metres – contradicting the advice given by the Highway Code!

Plus, if you want to get yourself on one of those TV documentary shows this is by far your best bet as the public just love to watch a good police pursuit. The best traffic officers would ticket (or 'knock of' to use the popular proverbial police term) their own grandma if her nearside rear brake light was out!

As well as showing an aptitude for traffic work, candidates for road policing positions have to show excellent driving prowess and car control. Coolness under pressure at chaotic multi-vehicle, serious injury accidents is a must. Traffic officers are also set specific targets each month and their performance is constantly monitored and scrutinised.

Then there's the dog section. A very desirable career choice and always fiercely contested when a spot on the team becomes available. The lonely dog handler patrols alone with only man's (or woman's) best friend to keep him/her company. Although tending to not be the most sociable of people, police dog handlers and their K9 colleagues are highly trained and can do amazing things at the right type of incident. A warning though – be wary of the scorned dog handler – if he/she finds out prior to his/her arrival you've walked all over the felon's path and therefore destroyed the 'track' the burglar took, they will not be best pleased and soon tell you about it!

A dog handler might have one, two or even three 4-legged friends at their disposal. All handlers will have a 'general purpose dog' (usually a larger breed like a German Shepherd) which can be used to track people, protect the handler and be deployed in public order situations. Contrary to what you see on TV (again), dogs cannot distinguish between one human and another; instead they can only track a human scent. So if there are too many other people walking around – referred to as 'foot traffic' – a police dog will not be effective. Other dogs are specialist K9's with exceptional senses of smell (Belgian Malinois, Labrador Retrievers, or even Springer Spaniels) trained to detect anything from narcotics, firearms, explosives, cash and even concealed cadavers. Dog handlers are highly self-motivated and serious candidates usually have a proven track record of proactive and high performance.

Maybe you are a thinking man's/woman's cop and CID is your ambition. Dealing with the most serious crimes that require meticulous investigation to send the more deviant criminals down – and all from the comfort of an office chair! The detective's arena is at the crime scene where attention to details pays dividends, as well as in the interview room where composed and decisive questioning will slowly unravel the webs of lies spun by the accused.

In order to climb the Investigation ladder aspiring officers must be prepared to work hard and be patient; starting in prisoner handling teams before showing the necessary ability to graduate to specialist investigation teams and maybe eventually major crime teams investigating the most high profile cases.

Alternatively you could get one of those police desk jobs

that readers of *The Daily Mail* are always complaining about; the ones who should be 'out on the streets' sorting out the hoody infestation in all the town centres across the land. In an ideal world all police officers would be patrolling all the time and catching the burglars and rapists and terrorists, not to mention stopping that Jack Russell from number 73 fowling the footpath again. But this is a bureaucratic world nowadays and if you're the type of bobby who wants to spend 33 of your 35 year police career hiding in a fluorescent-tube-lit, air-conditioned office at headquarters, then your local constabulary can even find a position for you! Although why you'd want to do this is beyond me.

Because I Want to Make a Difference

To stand up for the little guy, right? This is probably the correct answer, but you're going to have to come up with a weightier rationale to back it up, otherwise you'll sound like a one-dimensional Miss World contestant spouting that her ultimate desire is "world peace!" People will ask you "why?" all the time when they hear you've applied to be a police officer. I hope everyone who applies to join does so for the correct reasons. Ultimately the good officers do want to make the area they work in a safer place for its inhabitants. I do not work where my family or I live, but I work hard in the hope that in my home town another like-minded officer is doing the same to protect the ones I care about. There always seems to be hindrances being put in the way of front-line police; those obstacles can come from dim-witted senior officers who are out of touch with reality, an ineffective and antiquated judicial system, the government with ludicrous targets and league tables, or often just a lack of resourcing and funding.

But most of my colleagues, like myself, just get on with job at hand, do not moan or complain (much), and can hold their heads high knowing that, despite it all, we do our very best every shift. Nearly all police officers, myself included (as you're probably gathering), complain about the job all day long, but would we go back to doing a normal 9-to-5 job, with weekends off and half the stress we have now? Of course we wouldn't.

Whatever your reason, an exciting and challenging career awaits in service of the crown!

5. Training School

FACT: The National Policing Improvement Agency (NPIA) was formed in April 2007 with the remit of restructuring the way the police function through the training curriculum. They are responsible for the police application process, initial training and then ongoing training for all UK police forces.

With your application form approved, assessment centre a distant memory, medical passed and fitness test a doddle, you've finally got your start date and eagerly await your first day of training. Your uniform is fitted, your shirt is immaculate, the crease in the front of your trousers is bordering on being classed a bladed article and, having used a whole tin of Kiwi polish, your new boots are now bulled (polished/shined) to a standard that would make a brigadier weep with pride. Hopefully you haven't spent too much money on a pair of Special Forces tactical fighting gloves, a multi-tool knife approved by the British army, or a shock-sensitive watch that can summon the coastguard at the press of a button. *DO NOT* spend huge sums of cash on unnecessary kit – firstly you don't need it, and secondly experienced officers will laugh at you if you turn up with a utility belt like Batman's on your first day.

In years gone by, new recruits would be trained at large, regional training centres dotted around the country. These courses were residential and new recruits from all over were thrown together in an almost military style environment for several months before returning to their respective forces as lean, mean, law-enforcing machines. For economic reasons, as well as allowing them to be more hands-on with new recruits, forces now tend to do their own in-house training which is usually done at their HQ's. Wherever you train, one thing is for sure, mark my words: it will be nothing like those iconic *Police Academy* motion pictures from the 80's – as the real experience is filled with far more humour, joviality and frivolity!

Inevitably, if successful thus far, you will find yourself on day one sitting uncomfortably in a classroom full of equally perplexed strangers of all shapes and sizes. If the recruitment team have done their job and the right boxes have been ticked, your new best friends for the next six months or so should be a diverse mix of ages, races, sexualities and of course genders – a bit like the opening episode of *Big Brother*! For the next few months you'll be stuck in a small room being constantly tasked, challenged, observed and having your every word and action scrutinised – a bit like *Big Brother* – only it's the head of training you have to watch out for, not Davina. (Although I would still advise: "Please do not swear!")

I've compiled a Top 10 list of likely events that will happen during your training period involving you and your new brothers and sisters in law keeping. I can guarantee at least half a dozen of the following will happen during your time.

- At least two of your classmates will start a controversial relationship which will be kept secret for a maximum of one date.
- One class member will say and/or do something regretful and be invited to terminate their recent employment with immediate effect.
- Someone will burst into tears at regular intervals and half way through the course decide the police just isn't for them, resign, and go back to working in the police control room as a civilian.
- A rather annoying new colleague will have been a

special constable or PCSO before and speak like a 25-year veteran of the service believing he knows it all. Believe me, he doesn't.

- The quiet yet studious recruit won't say much and all the others will be convinced he/she is an undercover journalist trying to expose a secret racist culture among fresh constables. Keep an eye out for their hidden camera!

- You'll all go out for an alcohol-fuelled team-bonding evening excursion and someone will overdo it and embarrass themselves terribly – most likely by waving their shiny, new warrant card with the ink barely dry in the face of a doorman refusing them entry to the club (this might be linked to point 2 above).

- Someone will be injured during your self-defence training input and have to be put back a class as they recuperate.

- A chosen few will acquire new, unfortunate nicknames that will stick with them for their career.

- They'll be one weirdo that no one particularly likes or understands how he got this far along the process. Everyone else will try to avoid sitting with him for fear of being stuck with them in the endless group exercises. (This one is guaranteed, so if you're lucky enough to be at or even past this stage of the process, and now pondering in your head who the weirdo from your class might be but drawing a blank – maybe it was you?)

- An individual will inadvertently say or do something to greatly offend another individual in the same class. The offended will make an official complaint to a senior-ranked training officer, the whole atmosphere and group dynamic will change, and everyone else in the class will feel awkward and tense about the whole unfortunate mountain that started life as a tiny mole hill.

The Hard Sell

What sort of things can you expect to do during your training? As well as regularly sitting in a circle stating your name and telling those present "a little bit about yourself", during your first few weeks you'll probably find that various people from various departments and organisations will spend some time suggesting ways you can spend your newly earned police salary. People representing pensions, life insurance, personal accident cover and police social and sports clubs will all come to see you and offer you the opportunity to have lavish sums of money deducted from your earnings.

Although nowhere near as beneficial as some years ago, and also becoming increasingly expensive, the police pension is still a good one and pays out a lump sum and/or generous monthly payments should you reach the full 35 year term. Another recommendation would be joining the Police Federation; they are like a union working exclusively for rank-and-file police officers. In return for your monthly membership fee the Federation battles with the government as well as your own force every time they try to impose new harsh and unfair changes to the police service. On a personal level, each force has several Federation representatives who are always on hand to advise you about any matters causing you concern. The Federation will also stand by and assist you should you do something silly and get yourself in trouble.

FACT: All probationary police constables in England and Wales undertake an extensive and professional training program known as the Initial Police Learning and Development Program (IPLDP), leading to the Level 3 Diploma in Policing (QCF), during their first two years of service. The diploma replaces the previous NVQ in Policing Levels 3 and 4 qualification.

At some stage, usually early on in your training, you'll have the honour of being visited by a senior officer, or perhaps even your chief constable or commissioner if you're very fortunate! He or she will offer pearls of wisdom about how to channel your fresh enthusiasm towards a successful police career. Your chief officer must have done something right in their career to get to the top of the tree, so it might be wise to take heed of the knowledge and experience they impart. *On the other hand*, it will probably have been at least 20 years since they worked a night shift on the streets, and at least 10 years since they weren't surrounded by envious and fickle officers a rank or two below, desperately seeking promotion themselves, telling them how fantastic they are and how wonderful their new strategy to reduce police sickness is, etc. Regardless, make sure you sit up with your back straight, smile and nod politely, and agree with everything they say.

For many the police ranking system is a little hazy above Chief Inspector – fortunately senior ranks make it easy to tell them apart from the riff-raff (constables and sergeants) by wearing all manner of symbols and decorations on their shoulders – the more decoration and bling, the higher the rank. Basically if someone walks in the room with a picture of a crown or more embroidered on their epaulettes, make sure you stand up straight and call them 'Sir' or 'Ma'am' depending on their gender. (I am not going to tell you which gender correlates with which acknowledgment, but suffice to say if you get it wrong your career will be doomed from the outset!)

Heavy Lies the Crown

Another pep talk will come from your Professional Standards Department (PSD). This is what American films would refer to as *Internal Affairs*. The job of PSD is to ensure no officer falls foul of the many pitfalls out there. PSD are there to give guidance to naive officers who have, or are likely, to make foolish mistakes, and also to come down hard on corrupt coppers who tarnish the reputation of the hard-working police service. Listen intently to the advice they dispense, take everything on board, and then make it a goal to avoid contact with them ever again for the next 35 years. Most PSD officers are just doing a job and don't want to see officers young in service getting in trouble, but honesty and integrity must be paramount as previously stated. If the police are to punish people for wrongdoings and enforce the law, we ourselves must attain a high standard and be answerable should we fall below it.

In western society the foundations of justice are built on the principal of innocent until proven guilty – but not if you're a police officer though; remember, a griping member of the public can make an unsubstantiated complaint against an officer and, without a shred of evidence being presented by the complainant, PSD will be duty bound to investigate. Whilst doing so, the officer subject to that complaint can be moved to a different department, denied promotion, or even suspended from duty pending the outcome of the investigation. No one likes to see a colleague in trouble but police station gossip is rife with stories of witless or gullible officers who have done the most outrageous and monumentally stupid things to land themselves in hot water. These stories usually evolve and mutate into police folklore that echo through the ages as a warning to new officers of the perils out there – learn from the mistakes of others and steer clear of trouble.

Down to Business

The training itself will be comprehensive and thorough (hopefully). A procession of PowerPoint presentations coupled with more mnemonics and acronyms than you can shake a police baton at will leave your head spinning. You'll learn law, definitions, legislation, police powers and procedures. You'll also delve into mistakes made by the police in the past such as the Stephen Lawrence murder and subsequent MacPherson Report that concluded that the police are 'institutionally racist'; and the Victoria Climbie tragedy when the police failed to protect a young girl from her evil mother and step-father. It's important to understand why errors were made, and even more important to learn from mistakes so similar tragedies are avoided.

Training classes will also test an officer's moral fibre: do they have preconceived prejudices against certain elements of society? My colleagues and I may have our own opinions about class, sexuality, religion or even race, but this does not, and must not, affect how we treat any members of the public. I'm sure there are prejudiced and discriminatory police out there – fortunately I can hand-on-heart say I have never met any of them. On the street an officer's resolve and professionalism is tested to the extreme by people whose hate wants the officer to slip up, to give in, and to say or do something to leave themselves open to criticism. Your training and later experience in the field will teach you how to be resilient and not give way to decadence.

You can also expect a heavy input of 'Domestic And Honour-Based Violence'. These five words fill any experienced officer with dread. Not because the subject is not serious, relevant, or important, but because the Home Office dictates that a certain number of hours a year of a police officer's life MUST be filled with training dedicated to the subject. There are only so many times an officer can hear the same, repetitive, but still powerful statistics over and over again before his/her head explodes. I won't subject you to any 'DV' facts at this stage, but instead save those for later on in the book. (I am sure your anticipation is unbearable.)

At times the training can be a little confusing and the object of some lessons is not always clear: I remember one day at my HQ was spent writing as many swear words as we could think of on a white board. To this day I have no idea what the purpose of the exercise was, but even this was hugely beneficial because as a result I did add an infinite amount of new words to my everyday vocabulary!

I Have the Power

Police officers have special powers that mere civilians can only dream of. Not X-ray vision or telekinesis (although that would be cool) but powers to stop and search individuals, powers to use force, the power to seize certain items and the power to enter buildings to search for property and people to name but a few.

For example if a member of the public finds a house door ajar and enters to have a peek, he makes himself liable for arrest on suspicion of burglary.

However, as a police officer in the same circumstances you have a power under Section 17 of PACE to enter to save life and limb as you will of course be concerned for the welfare of any persons that might be contained inside, right?

We'll talk more about police powers as this book goes on but here is your first example:

POWER: Section 17 of the Police And Criminal Evidence Act (PACE) 1984 states a police constable may enter a premises (by force is necessary) to effect the arrest of a subject for an indictable (imprisonable) offence as long as they have reasonable grounds to believe the subject is inside; or to enter a premises to 'save life and limb' should they have serious concerns for the wellbeing of a person inside.

If you have a good knowledge of these powers it will aid you in your duty and make you a far more effective officer. It will also allow you to better justify your actions when they're called into question by disgruntled prisoners and defence solicitors, so make sure you pay attention.

TOP TIP: The police's powers to stop and search individuals are a contentious issue and regularly enter the media spotlight. When used properly these powers are one of the most effective tools in a street cop's arsenal. Learn them well to operate effectively, as well as to ensure your integrity is beyond reproach.

Welcome to Fight Club

Fortunately, the monotony of the seemingly endless PowerPoint procession is broken up by self-defence training in the gym. As well as learning all manner of pain-compliance holds that you can try out on friends, family and later on uncooperative members of the public (strictly in the course of your duty you understand), you'll also be introduced to your PPE (personal protection equipment) which consists of the following:

Handcuffs – The days of cuffs with links of chain in the middle are long gone. Forces now use cuffs with a rigid centre as this is designed to prevent escape and also injury to the person wearing them, whilst still allowing the officer control over their prisoner. Some forces have funky cuffs that fold in the middle for easier storage when not in use. You'll be taught the latest Home Office approved cuffing techniques and get the chance to try them out on unsuspecting classmates. Your body and particularly wrists will ache for days afterwards I can promise you. Prisoners often complain that cuffs are secured on them too tight. They seem unconsoled when it is pointed out to them the cuffs are not designed for comfort.

TOP TIP: Instead of the shock resistant watch that calls the coastguard, purchasing a long cuff key from any police kit web site would be a far wiser investment (available from £5 upwards). The shiny new cuffs issued by the stores department tend to only come with a short, stumpy cuff key that is fiddly to use, especially when in real world situations. Keep the short key somewhere on your person as a spare though. Also a decent – but not extravagant – LED torch is an advisable purchase too (from £25 upwards) if not already issued by your force.

Incapacitant Spray – Some forces use CS (or 2-

chlorobenzalmalononitrile to use its chemical name) spray whilst others use PAVA (pelargonic acid vanillylamide). Both are technically Section 5 firearms (you'll learn all about firearms and their definitions) and can't be legally owned by members of the public in this country, although readily available on the continent. Either has the power to reduce a full grown, snarling, angry man to a blubbering, choking, snot monster at the press of the cap. CS in particular tends to turn everyone unfortunate enough to be in the immediate proximity when discharged into a blubbering, snot monster, irrespective of whether they're wearing a uniform or not, so please bear this in mind. They work by affecting the eyes and exposed skin, especially the nose and throat. When first introduced new recruits were sprayed with a diluted dose so they could experience the sensation in a controlled training environment. This practice has since ceased as a small percentage of people are allergic and it makes their heads swell up like the elephant man; no point in damaging a perfectly good recruit that early on in their training I guess!

Of course you'll be given full instruction on this and get to have water fights with exact replica cans filled with something far less harmful.

Baton – Again forces vary on their standard-issue baton. Most have the extendable, friction-lock baton usually manufactured by a company called ASP (Armament Systems and Procedures). This is a telescopic baton which works by flicking out the handle, causing the shaft to lock in place, and has a small metal stud at the end. This type of baton is collapsed by bashing the end on a solid, thick surface (like the pavement I mean, not an offenders head).

The other type of baton is the side-handle baton

(sometimes referred to as T-batons or nightsticks). These are batons with a short side handle at a right angle to the shaft, about six inches from one end; a bit more cumbersome as they don't retract, but arguably more versatile – especially when used to defend.

Giving your handcuff and baton a girl's name is optional.

Taser – Don't get excited just yet! You will NOT be issued a taser straight away. Most forces have only issued these to firearms and traffic officers. Following successful trials, some forces have extended this to specially trained divisional officers, but none hand them out to brand new recruits just yet! The police issue zapper of choice is currently the taser X26 which can be used at distances of up to 26 feet, but is most effective between 7 to 12 feet. It fires a pair of barbs on copper wires that embed themselves in the suspect's clothing (or bare, tattooed skin) and sends out an electrical current of 50,000 volts.

The shock can cause temporary loss of muscle control or 'neurological muscular incapacitation', making the target fall to the ground or freeze on the spot. However, in most cases the ominous sight of a little red dot on the subject's chest has the desired effect of achieving compliance without the need for discharge.

FACT: In the 1970's a man called Jack Cover, a NASA scientist and former WW2 bomber pilot, discovered that low voltage electric current alternately pulsed with high voltage could generate rapid muscle contractions, thereby immobilising a human being. He named his invention a taser, an acronym for Thomas A. Swift's Electric Rifle. Ironically Thomas A. Swift was the scientist's favourite fictional comic book character – only in America!

During this part of the syllabus, officers are also trained in basic first aid, but don't expect to be equipped with the skills to perform an emergency tracheotomy with only a hollow biro pen. In truth the training provided is on par with that which a cub scout might need to pass their first aid badge or what you might learn by watching a few episodes of *Casualty*. Fortunately, due to the health and safety obsession we have in modern society, there are always members of the public on hand who are qualified office first-aiders to tell you what to do should you stumble across a collapsed pensioner outside Debenhams.

You'll punch and kick pads, hit stuff with your batons, and throw your new colleagues around like they're villainous scum. You probably don't even know where your mandibular nerve is right now, but you soon will. Even if you do know where it is I bet you've never had a person painfully thrust the side of their index finger into it before – something to look forward to. After you've demonstrated and been assessed, at the end of your 'Personal Safety Training' course you'll officially have a self-defence ticket, not to mention having the moves of Jean Claude Van Damme (though sadly they don't show you how to do the splits between two chairs).

POWERS: The following legislation governs police 'Use of Force' and it is very important for officers to have a good understanding of each. The important bits of each legislation are briefly summarised for you:

Human Rights Act 1984

Every human (even those belonging to the Butcher family, who you will hear of later) have the right to life, as well as to live that life free from torture.

Common Law (not an 'Act', instead historic law developed by judges sitting in courts over centuries).

Everyone has the right to defend themselves by using 'reasonable force' (emphasis on the 'reasonable' part). This power allows the police – and in fact any member of the public too – to make 'pre-emptive strikes', i.e. to hit (or cover with incapacitant spray, or taser, or even baton) a would-be attacker first as long as it is justifiable.

Section 3 Criminal Law Act 1967

This power also applies to everyone, not just those holding the Office of Constable; it grants the power to use 'reasonable force' to prevent crime and when necessary make an arrest.

Section 117 Police And Criminal Evidence Act (PACE) 1984

This one applies to police officers only. It gives officers the power to use 'reasonable force' (you should be spotting a recurring theme here) to execute their duties within the rest of PACE, such as Section 1 'Stop and Searches' (to be discussed later) for example.

Care in the Community

Another memorable experience from my days at training school was the community placement. To bring new officers into contact with future clientele they usually endure two weeks working within an employer or organisation that assists the less fortunate (or in some cases the downright criminal). It reminded me of being 15 years old again and doing work experience – only this time they didn't try to send me out for tins of tartan paint or left handed screwdrivers. Also, I didn't need my mum to pick me up at the end of each day.

The placements are typically at locations like charity organisations, housing associations, community groups or maybe you'll even spend a couple of weeks with the heroes at the second emergency service – the fire brigade! Mine was at an inner city night shelter. Arriving for my first shift in plain clothes and unrecognisable as a 'rozzer', I was greeted by a sign warning visitors about a scabies epidemic sweeping the shelter. Nice. My first night was spent preparing food for intoxicated people, helping drug addicts wash faeces from their clothes, and assisting a female to look through some old donated garments to replace the ones she'd just urinated in. Day two was much easier though as someone had made an anonymous tip-off that a police officer had infiltrated the shelter so nobody wanted me to help them with anything – I was less popular than the contagious skin disease.

Despite the difficult working conditions I left the shelter at the end of the two weeks equipped with a new and eye-opening realisation of how some unfortunates live their lives. Even better – I had also not caught scabies! I had great admiration for the staff at the shelter who did a fantastic job and received little thanks in return for all their efforts. This was my first glimpse of how the other half live. A hard-as-nails, 30-year veteran once told me in this job you meet three kinds of people – the mad, the bad, and the sad. These poor people were definitely the latter.

On the Job

At the end of the training segment student officers are shipped off to a tutor unit where experienced officers will put hopefuls through their paces in real-life jobs, on real-life streets and with real-life members of the public. Although protected, constantly observed and mentored continuously, new officers will finally get a taste of what a real police officer does. They won't have you tackling knife-wielding maniacs or crushing multi-million-pound drug cartels in week one (that comes in week two), but you will be slowly introduced into real-world policing that is impossible to replicate in a classroom.

Whilst in their tutorship, instructors will endeavour to give officers an insight into all the fundamental and basic tasks asked of a front-line officer. This will include attending incidents, speaking with victims and witnesses, arresting offenders, interviewing, as well as inherent and basic investigation. No doubt there will also be a training input on how to make three cups of tea with only one tea bag and the milk stealthily stolen from the admin department's fridge – an invaluable skill indeed.

By this stage of the training an enthusiastic recruit should be getting very excited as they are so close to making it to the big show. Like most things in life you only get out what you put it, so take the opportunity to learn from the tutors and ask as many questions as you can. The downfall of many a headstrong probationer is actually over confidence, sometimes bordering on arrogance. Until now training has been pink, fluffy and conducted in a replicated but sterile and protected environment at headquarters. Some newbies will think they already know it all as they've done so well at 'knowledge checks' in the classroom or shone in self-defence training with their magnificent arm-entanglement take-down. Pride comes before a fall in this job so remain humble, volunteer for everything, and extract all that you can from the proficient people around you.

Some of what you learn is interesting, some is challenging, some is even exciting, and naturally some is mind-numbingly boring, but try to absorb as much as you can. Don't be too daunted if not all goes in at first though, as most of what you need to know can only be learnt working in the real world. The training school environment is a kind of parallel universe where best practice is preached, standard operating procedures are always adhered to, the law is black and white with no grey in between, and political correctness rules supreme. The militant environment can seem oppressive and disconcerting at times. I remember once being told we don't do 'brainstorm diagrams' any more, as this could be offensive to people with mental health issues! Presumably an unfortunate individual's brain was once actually 'stormed' – most likely by overexposure to domestic violence training – and this is now deemed a discriminatory term. Instead we now do 'spider graphs' – I pointed out this might be offensive to our arachnid friends, but was told by the trainer to desist from being facetious or the Chief Inspector would hear of my insubordination.

The real world is nothing like training school, but corner cutting can lead to bad practices, ineffective investigation, poor results and unhappy victims – not to mention possible disciplinary actions – so try to absorb as much of your training as you can as this is the foundation on which to build your skills.

Not that corner cutting is necessarily a bad thing or that good officers don't do it; it's just that until you have the experience to know which corners can be cut and how, you leave yourself open to criticism. As your knowledge and skills develop you'll realise that, as long as it doesn't undermine the service you provide, not only is corner cutting acceptable but in fact an essential part of day-to-day policing. If everything is done 'by the book' you'll never have enough time to do everything that is demanded of you working as a front-line officer.

6. Welcome to Division

10 things not to say on your first day:

- I can't wait to finally get out there and crack some skulls!
- Why don't they make the hot WPC's wear skirts any more?
- With all this police intelligence and systems, there must be a way to find out that girl's phone number from Saturday night.
- I'm an undercover reporter for The Sun.
- Dude, I was so drunk last night, I don't know how I drove here this morning!
- So when do we get the guns?
- Do we really have to seize *all* this money? I'm sure if we get our stories straight we can keep a little for ourselves.
- No-one will talk down to me now I'm a cop. I'll show them all who's a sissy now!
- Everyone's tried cannabis before. I don't understand why it's illegal. Where is the drugs safe by the way?
- Half the people in this job are only here because they ticked a box, you know.

Finally, having studied for several months, you're at a stage where optimistically – and only under strict supervision – will you no longer present a great risk to yourself, members of the public and – most importantly – the reputation of your police force. You are a student police constable. You are ready for 'Division'. Divisional police officers are the infantry, the front-line – they are the non-specialised officers who make up the response officer teams as well as, in most forces, the local policing teams (sometimes referred to as safer neighbourhood teams).

Response

Whether your force refers to them as 'Response', 'First Contact', 'Intervention' or whatever – their role is the same: response officers deal with emergency calls and take responsibility for jobs requiring a quick attendance. They will arrive at incidents, having the first contact with the public and quickly establish what has happened, what offences (if any) have taken place, who are the victims, who are witnesses and who are offenders/suspects. If possible and applicable, arrests will be made. The primary investigation (sometimes referred to as 'the golden hour period') will also be completed by the response team under guidance of senior rank. This will mean gathering the evidence that is essential to the criminal investigation and doing so as quickly as possible so that it is not lost, contaminated or corrupted. That evidence might be a forensic scene that needs preserving for scenes of crime officers (SOCO) or crime scene investigators (CSI); weapons or property that need seizing; or statements from victims and witnesses that need taking. Being a response officer should be what most applicants imagine and strive to be when employed as a new recruit.

Local Policing Team

The remit of local policing will involve dealing with community issues and tensions. Although not as glamorous a role as being a traffic or firearms officers, or perhaps even that of the response officers, local policing is still a vitally important part in serving the tax-paying public (and of course the non-tax-paying public as some just don't feel like working). The majority of normal people read the papers, watch the news, and vigorously shake their heads in a disapproving manner at the stories of gangland members shooting each other in the city, the millions of pounds of profit lost by supermarkets as a result of shoplifters, the corruption in Westminster, or even the spate of burglaries in the estate on the other side of town. They do not like it and something should be done about it, damn it! *But* ultimately they won't be losing any sleep over it.

What they *will* however have huge concerns over are the hoodies shouting, swearing, drinking and spitting at the end of their road. They *will* care about the cars parked illegally by commuters outside their house Monday to Friday. They *will* be furious about the youths riding their mini-motos on the fields at the back of their 3-bed semi. And they *will* demand immediate capital punishment for anyone from the Chavington Manor Estate caught littering KFC wrappers on their award-winning front lawn! This is where the local policing team comes in – sorting out these matters and providing an invaluable service to the community.

People sometimes ask me (usually the elderly if I'm honest, just after they've commented that police officers seem to be getting so much younger nowadays) why they don't see 'bobbies on the beat' anymore. The truthful answer is it's a huge waste of resources – although it might be reassuring to see a male and female officer plodding the cobbles together down the pedestrianised shopping precinct like on the closing credits of *The Bill*, unless a crime is committed right in front of them they will struggle to be an effective resource. In this tight economic time officers on foot beat are an expensive luxury that cannot be afforded –

instead police community support officers (PCSOs) who do not have the same police powers, do not require the same levels of training and, as a result are paid marginally less wages, are the preferred (by politicians) alternative option for a high visibility presence on the streets.

Hello Shifts, Goodbye Social Life!

Having completed the final part of training under your tutor you will be allocated a station to work from and a 'shift' of officers to work with. Once again you will find yourself sitting in a room full of strangers feeling awkward, most likely a little inadequate, with the knowledge and wisdom you acquired at training school slowly seeping from your mind. The majority of the confidence built up over your training and tutor period will shortly be destroyed as the reality of being a real cop on the front-line hits home hard. Most officers will admit from time to time in their first few months on the streets they felt overawed and unprepared – I know I did. Do not be disheartened if this happens, you will overcome it as your experience and skills grow and you learn from your new colleagues.

A team of officers is called a 'section' or 'shift' (or sometimes just 'team'). The shift will consist of a number of police constables (PC's) and at least one police sergeant (PS's) or so. The number of sergeants will depend on the size of the shift and ratio of PC's. Sitting at the top of the shift Christmas tree is the police inspector – 'the guvnor' (ranks above 'Inspector' work far more social hours and will rarely venture out of their offices unless there is a very serious incident unfolding – or if they are playing golf that afternoon with other senior officers). No doubt your merry band will be made up of very different characters with varying levels of experience and expertise and all with their own unique quirks and working habits.

There is no national standard shift pattern or rota, instead just guidelines offered by the Home Office; each force will have its own shift pattern that suits their policing needs and resources best. Generally speaking, an average shift pattern will consist of a rotation of early (or day) shifts, late shifts (sometimes referred to as 'back shift') and night shifts. Sometimes shifts are referred to as 'tours of duty'. 'Earlies' will indeed start very early and finish sometime in the afternoon; 'lates' will commence in the afternoon and end late at night; whilst night shifts will – you guessed it – run throughout the night until the early shift takes over. A number of sections/shifts/teams (usually five) will complete the shift pattern. There will be enough shifts to allow for three of them to be working the three shift types (i.e. early, late and night) each day of the week, whilst allowing those not working to have sufficient time off (or rest days) between work. Each section/shift/team's working hours that day will generally overlap each other, especially at busiest times such as Friday and Saturday nights.

Below is a simplified example of a typical 5-week shift pattern:

	Mon	Tue	Wed	Thur	Fri	Sat	Sun
W 1	2100-0700	2100-0700	2100-0700	2100-0700	RD	RD	RD
W 2	0700-1500	0700-1500	0700-1700	RD	RD	1700-0300	1400-0000
W 3	1400-0000	1400-0000	RD	RD	2100-0700	2100-0700	2200-0700
W 4	RD	RD	RD	0700-1700	0700-1700	0700-1700	0700-1500
W 5	RD	RD	1400-0000	1400-0000	1700-0300	RD	RD

In the above example each of the five shifts will be working one of the five weeks. For example, if the first team (let's call them A Shift) are working week 1, B Shift will be working week 2, C Shift week 3 and so on. On Monday, B Shift will be working the early shifts (7 a.m. to 3 p.m.), C Shift the late shifts (2 p.m. until midnight) and A Shift the night shifts (9 p.m. until 7 a.m.); whilst D and E Shifts have the day off (the lucky buggers!)

You'll note throughout the 5 weeks, the 'late shift' hours are the most variable as they are tailored to cover the peak 'public order' (drunken idiots) times at weekends.

There's no doubt about it, shift work can be hard and have a huge impact on an individual officer's welfare, not to mention their family and friends. Bank holidays and seasonal or religious celebrations have no relevance in the police shift rotation. When most people go out to play – such as long bank holiday weekends, the festive period and New Year's Eve – all the emergency services are stretched to the limits, so even annual leave is hard to come by.

FACT: Being late off work is a common occurrence for police officers. Usually it is unavoidable and as soon as new recruits accept this, the better. Police officers do not get paid for the first half hours overtime; it is a long tradition that the first additional thirty minutes of an officer's shift are given freely to her majesty, hence it is known as 'The Queen's Half Hour'. Unplanned overtime after this first half hour will be paid.

Meet the Team

One of the best things about my job is the people I work with. The camaraderie and banter at police stations is why many officers come to work with an occasional smile on their faces. Can you imagine working with a group of like-minded people, all open-minded and not easily offended, hard-working and motivated, accepting, tolerant and non-judgmental, committed to a common goal and striving to make the world a better place? No, neither can I; but the motley crew I work with are nearly as gratifying.

I don't get on with all my colleagues, in fact there are some I'd go as far as to say I don't like (and they probably don't like me), but most I consider good friends. Having a tight group of officers is not only important on a professional level but equally important on an emotional one too. I know my crew mate will put himself/herself in harm's way to protect me, and he/she knows I'll do the same in return. Whatever happens in the future I know I have made friends for life and we all support each other at those difficult times.

Each working day starts with a briefing where the team of officers meet or 'parade on'. The sergeant will discuss the day's duties, dispense arrest attempts to be tried by the fortunate chosen ones, and dish out 'cell watches' to hapless others. Since cell watches are a regular pastime of the student officer, I'll briefly explain.

Certain prisoners are incapable of conducting themselves like normal human beings and instead behave like spoilt children (even when approaching what would be justly deemed middle age). Certain scroats require an officer to constantly observe them otherwise they will try to hang themselves with their underwear, smash their skull on the cell wall, or try to eat their own faeces. Even a cell with CCTV fitted is insufficient protection sometimes. So an officer will be required to sit on a chair, just outside the cell door, gazing emotionlessly at the freak of nature within, desperately trying to not make eye contact for fear of having to engage in conversation with them. This is a regular occurrence in custodies up and down the country and, as you might imagine, places a huge strain on resources not to mention wasting taxpayer's money. Often the well-seasoned prisoner will play up sufficiently in custody so they are placed on a cell watch just so they have someone to wind away the hours in custody with – or at least until they fall asleep; although this is no reprieve for the officer as they still have to remain attentively just outside the cell in case they wake up again. Cell watches are a rite of passage that every officer must undertake – especially in their early career.

Back to the briefing: once the unpleasantries of cell watch assignments are over, it's on to the intelligence briefing where officers get an insight into what's going on in their patrol area – police officers don't just drive around randomly between doughnut shops and coffee stops, don't you know! Intelligence officers amalgamate various data at the police's disposal and condense it all down into a package for patrol officers to absorb so they can make best use of that most rare and precious commodity – time on the streets to patrol.

The PowerPoint theme from training school usually continues here as the shift of officers parading on goes through numerous slides of text and accompanying mug shots of the local dregs of society and recent events. It seems in most cases criminals are particularly unattractive people with poor personal hygiene – it could be said that some have faces only a mother could love (that is assuming they're not on the briefing for robbing their own mothers for cash to buy heroin). In my local town the premier crime family are the Butchers.

They all live together in a 4-bedroom detached house, provided for them by the local council on behalf of the taxpayer, on the Chavington Manor Estate. Their house is easily identifiable – it's the one with a stripped out Ford Capri on the driveway, various abandoned white goods on the over grown lawn, garish Christmas decorations still up on the porch roof (even though it's now mid-July) and discarded food containers spilling out onto the street at the front. If you peek through the gaps in the newspapers stuck to the windows in lieu of curtains, in the living room you'll see hanging on their wall a 52" LED TV. There's Daddy Butcher, Mummy Butcher, the two Brothers Grimm Butcher, and finally there's darling Daughter Butcher. The Butcher family are almost definitely humanoid but barely human. They have mastered walking upright and with their opposable thumbs can even use primitive tools, such as TV remotes and bricks to smash car windows, which sets them apart from their close primate cousins. The whole family singlehandedly prove Darwin's theory of evolution as each one resembles the missing link. None of them have ever done an honest day's work in all their lives – they symbolise all that is wrong with 'Broken Britain' and not a day goes by that at least one, or often all of them, doesn't appear on the briefing having been arrested for, suspected of, or wanted for a recently committed crime. Pond life.

The intelligence that generates the briefing comes from various sources, but most often starts with intelligence reports from the front-line officers themselves. Being the ones on the street and therefore most in contact with the criminal underclass makes the 'intel' front-line officers can gather invaluable. This might come from simple rumours that emanate from the local grapevine, or by officer Stop/Checks of known offenders to the police. With experience a good officer will recognize and even build some kind of rapport with the local villains. When this happens you will be amazed what little titbits fickle rogues are prepared to give away about their fellow criminals. Naturally some undesirables are dishonest and tell lies to the police – hard to believe I know – but the savvy officer can usually sort the wheat from the chaff.

TOP TIP: You'll soon realise the same names crop up all the time, over and over again. People regularly involved in crime are referred to as 'nominals'. Whether they're offenders, victims or witnesses, it's no exaggeration to say 80% of the police's time is taken up by 20% of the population. If you get chance to have a look at some of these nominals in the flesh – perhaps in custody or when they attend the station as part of their bail conditions – try to do so as they do not always look like their mug shots. It will pay dividends when you come across them on the streets next time.

It's My First Time

Making your first arrest seems a very big deal at the time. I have heard officers compare it to your first kiss; this is a fairly accurate comparison – lots of trepidation and anticipation, ultimately satisfying, but really you are just glad to have gotten it out of the way (although luckily my first arrest wasn't of a young female with acne, NHS glasses, braces and wearing a t-shirt with East 17's tour dates on the back). Don't worry when the first time you apprehensively mumble the police caution at a culprit and it all comes out gobbledygook. I sounded a complete imbecile, incapable of forming any sentence, the first time I attempted to stutter the necessary words to take a detained shoplifter's liberty away and arrest them.

When new to division, throw yourself in and volunteer for everything. Get a few arrests under your belt and rely on your training. Watch and learn from experienced colleagues and don't be afraid to make honest mistakes – it's all part of the learning process and as said before you get out of this job what you put into it. Most of all enjoy it – this is what you wanted and signed up for!

7. Thievery

FACT: Shoplifting costs retailers in the UK £4.4 billion a year and this results in an increase of £180 a year on an average family's annual shopping bill to cover this loss in profits. Source: June 2010 survey carried out by retail security company Checkpoint Systems

So you're now through your basic training and somehow you're a front-line police officer! What can you expect to be doing with your time? (It's not all coffee and doughnuts you know.) I'd like to go into what a police officer does and give illustrations of everyday scenarios that an officer might find themselves in so that you know what to expect. Let's start with theft incidents.

Ever since Adam and Eve cohabited the Garden of Eden, theft has been a problem – although the Almighty's sentencing guidelines are much stricter than those used by the courts of today. A theft is a police officer's bread and butter job. If you only learn one offence definition, make it this one:

A person is guilty of theft, if he dishonestly appropriates property belonging to another with the intention of permanently depriving the other of it.

I said I wouldn't go into definitions and law too much because that's not what this book is about, but imagine how impressed your trainer will be if you already know this one before they show you it on the projector screen in their PowerPoint presentation.

Put simply, something has been stolen if a baddy

takes an item that he knows he is not entitled to, that belongs to someone else, and he doesn't ever intend to give back. A lot of jobs a new student officer will deal with will be theft related offences; whether they be thefts from shops, thefts from people, thefts from vehicles, robberies or burglaries. The latter two are more serious offences and most police forces will have specialist teams who deal with them, but even then front-line police officers will most likely be expected to attend crime scenes in the first instance, speak with victims and witnesses, gather evidence and – if you're lucky – arrest the offender(s).

I don't want to go too much in to the technical side of offences and legislation as again that is not the intention of this book. You will be sufficiently equipped with this information by your trainers. I would however like to give you some examples of typical situations you may find yourself in when employed as a police constable.

Meet Geoffrey Steeles. Geoff is a white male, aged in his mid-60's (but looks even older), approximately 5'8" tall, medium build and with grey, scruffy hair on both his balding head and chin. Geoff is a style icon, although his preferred outfit in recent times is a relatively conservative tweed jacket with leather patches on the elbows, a shirt with a collar, tracksuit bottoms that finish six inches above his ankles and leather sandals on his feet to complete the look. Geoff most famously once wore a fur coat and full wetsuit ensemble – complete with snorkel and flippers – whilst trying to steal a microwave oven from Lidl! (He was unsuccessful.) His dress sense is the stuff of legend in the town but until the Crimes Against Fashion Act of 2013 is passed by parliament and Geoff is wanted by the Fashion Police, we cannot hold his appearance against him. His fashion sense is not Geoff's biggest problem though, oh no; Geoff is absent minded: he keeps forgetting to pay for goods at shops. In fact, it's fair to say Geoff has not grasped the concept of shopping at all as the simple concept of exchanging money in return for goods is completely lost on him.

Unlike most thieves, Geoff doesn't have a habit to support; he doesn't do drugs, he doesn't drink excessively, *but* he does have an addiction. Geoff's demon is that he loves the buzz of pilfering items from shops. Sadly, he also enjoys prison food and masculine company, so the prospect of spending six weeks or so at Her Majesty's pleasure every so often for a few minor indiscretions is no problem at all to him and an occupational hazard he gleefully accepts. Mr Steeles is institutionalised and if he spends too long at liberty in the free world he starts to yearn for the security of an 8-by-10 foot prison cell and three meals a day guaranteed. For him prison is a bit like Butlins with bars. No retailer is safe from this one-man crime spree. As well as being acquainted with every police officer in town, he is also well known to all store security guards, not to mention all the town CCTV operators.

One Tuesday afternoon, I'm out patrolling my normal routes thinking how 'Q' the day has been. (Police officers never say the word 'Quiet' as it is scientifically proven that that the slightest mention of that word instantly brings about a sexual offences job, and nothing strikes more fear into a police officer than the thought of dealing with one of those!) If I am lucky I might even get off duty on time for a change.

Suddenly the tranquillity is broken when my radio crackles to life and the control room ask me to attend the supermarket where *every little helps*. I ask them to pass details and I'm told a 70-year-old white male has been detained by security after trying to leave the store with unpaid for packets of meat and cheese. My thoughts turn to the enigmatic Geoffrey instantly and I tell the control room I am en route.

As I park my shiny police car outside the store and make my way to the entrance, I see a tracksuit-clad woman and her three-year-old infant staring at me as I pass.

I hear the mother playfully say to her son, "Look Kieran, the policeman's here to take you away 'coz you've been naughty!"*

The mother grins. The son recoils from me with terror and holds his parent's hand tighter. Normally I would lecturer the woman and point out being the 'bogey-man' is not the image the modern 21st century police service tries to portray to small, young, impressionable children, but today I'm eager to see what fashion faux pas Geoffrey's sporting.

Instead I smile at the young man and cheerfully say, "Hi, mate, how you doing? I'm sure you're a good lad really."

The boy takes another step back and starts to cry so I quickly enter the store.

*Mothers, the police do not take naughty children away! Please stop telling your kids this as it is not helpful when millions of pounds are spent nationwide on school campaigns to make the police more approachable to today's youth. Anyway, it's actually Social Services that take naughty children away from their families. (Although it's often on our advice though. Ahem.)

I make my way into the security holding room and there sits a familiar, glum-looking old man with two security guards either side. Attire-wise I'm not disappointed as today Geoffrey has made a real effort and sports a deerstalker hat, sunglasses, obligatory tweed jacket under which is a bright yellow t-shirt with a semi-offensive slogan emblazoned across the front, an 80's neck tie with the image of a kipper printed on it, and, in lieu of his usual tracksuit bottoms that are shy of his ankles, he instead wears green, cotton trousers that look suspiciously like the ones issued to prisoners in police station custodies when we seize their clothes. His beard is particularly wiry and dishevelled today with what looks like cornflakes matted into it. The sandals survived his makeover and are wrapped around his dirty, hairy, hobbit-like toes. A visual treat to behold as ever!

"Morning Geoffrey, how are you today?"

"P*ssed off actually. I want to make a complaint," he replies.

"Oh really?" I can't help but find his last statement the tiniest bit ironic. "What about?"

"Assault. These two apes gripped me up and shoved me around." He looks up with resentment at the two security officers rolling their eyes and shaking their heads.

"Was that because you were up to your old tricks again?" I query.

The security officer on the left interrupts. "He's banned from the store already. He came in and we saw him on CCTV pick up the meat and cheese, put it in his jacket and then try to walk out. We challenged him at the exit and brought him in here."

Because Geoffrey is already banned from the store, he has technically burgled it this time as he entered as a trespasser, but in my experience the Crown Prosecution Service will never run with that. Geoff is indeed banned from this store – but then he is also banned from every branch of every major retailer in the United Kingdom. In fact if he was to adhere to all his store-banning orders, he would probably have to travel to a small, independent store outside of a 50-mile radius of the town he lives in to find one he hasn't stolen from yet, and subsequently been banned from, just to purchase a pot noodle.

POWER: Under Section 1 of the Police And Criminal Evidence (PACE) Act 1984, a police officer may search any person or attended vehicle for stolen goods, weapons, or implements made or adapted for use in crime as long as they have reasonable grounds for suspecting the subject may be in possession of said items. This is commonly referred to as powers of 'Stop and Search'.

I'm now shaking my head disapprovingly at Geoff and ask, "So have you got any stolen goods on you? I'm going to search you."

"Nope," is the blasé reply, "I'm not into that thievery malarkey." A greater untruth has never before been uttered.

"OK, stand up for me."

As he reluctantly stands a packet of beef fillets and a tube of toothpaste fall out from under his jacket.

"What's that, Geoff?" I quizzically ask staring at the previously concealed goods.

Geoff shrugs his shoulders and says, "Dunno."

The shrugging causes a bag of frozen chicken dippers to also fall to the floor.

With a sigh I search Geoff and find what amounts to a weekly shop for most families totalling

£60:02 secreted about his person. With the stolen goods laid out on a table, I grab a quick snap of the bounty on my police Blackberry as prosecutors love evidential photographs that might be later used in court, because of course 'a picture paints a thousand words', before the perishable goods can be returned to the shelves.

"OK, Geoff. You know the score; I'm going to have to arrest you for theft. I'm going to caution you now – so join in with the words if you know it." Taking a deep breath: "You do not have to say anything, however it may harm your defence if you do not mention when questioned something that you later rely on in court. Anything you do say may be given in evidence."

An officer should note down any immediate reply to the caution, however in this case Geoff merely makes a grunting noise. As I do not possess the literary prowess to formulate that sound into a word, I make no record of it in my pocket notebook. The final formality upon arresting a person is to inform them of the necessity to arrest them there and then. In this case – as in most cases – the necessity is for a 'prompt and effective investigation'. There are other 'necessity codes' (reasons to arrest) but I will not bore you with them here.

Geoff declines the invitation to join me in caution karaoke, but does accompany me on the walk back to my car. Shoppers turn and watch as I lead Geoff away in handcuffs. For most this would be an incredibly shameful experience, but Geoff doesn't even flutter an eyelid as women tut disapprovingly and shake their heads vigorously as we parade past. Little Kieran takes a step behind his mother once more as I pass by.

The security officers escort us from the premises, before returning to their posts. As they do I call back to remind them to make me a copy of the CCTV, as well as produce a receipt for the total value of goods stolen, as I'll be back to collect them both once Geoff is safely back at the police station where for a few hours at least he will no longer be a menace to the town's shopkeepers.

After arresting him, via my radio I run a Police National Computer check on Geoff which reveals he has previously been arrested a whopping 395 times, which means he has heard the police caution more times than I have actually said it. Several minutes of radio air-time are taken up as the police radio controller passes me all of Geoff's bail conditions for the seven other pending offences he is already on bail for. I'm also informed he has the obligatory 'VIOLENT' PNC marker.

On the journey back to the nick and away from the security officers who he believes so violently assaulted him, Geoff is much more talkative. We don't talk about the circumstances around his most recent memory lapse as that must wait for the tape-recorded interview, but Geoff is happy to tell me about why there are no incentives for him to cease his maverick ways and also treats me with a rundown on which are his favourite prisons. Geoff has after all at some time or another been a guest in most of the jails in England, so is excellently placed to give his opinion. Apparently there is an open prison in Essex which is Geoff's preferred vacation destination at this time as they now have a fantastically refurbished recreation room for the benefit of the inmates – I am sure it is of great relief for all taxpayers to know that the boredom of lodgers at that particular prison has been addressed.

FACT: 60% of those released from prison re-offend within the first year. More than 70% of prisoners admit using drugs in the 12 months before their incarceration. An alarming 7% said they tried heroin for the very first time whilst in prison. Source: Ministry of Justice survey of prisoners 2010.

When we arrive in the police station yard, Geoff and I make the short and familiar walk for both of us to the custody gate which is opened by the civilian detention officer (DO).

"Morning Geoff," the DO says.

Geoff just nods. We approach the custody desk and are greeted by the custody sergeant.

"Morning Geoff," the custody sergeant says.

"Any chance of a fag, boss?" Geoff optimistically asks.

Smoking anywhere in police stations was outlawed in 2007 at the same time as the English smoking ban in public places came into effect. Not being able to smoke is often the biggest inconvenience of being arrested for many regular police custody suite visitors. Geoff is instead offered various forms of nicotine replacement therapy, which ironically costs the taxpayer far more than if he was just given his own cigarettes to smoke.

The custody suite is the domain of the custody sergeant and he/she has ultimate responsibility for the welfare of prisoners whilst in their care. Every time a prisoner is brought into custody, the grounds are given to the sergeant in charge so that he/she can decide if they will accept the prisoner for what will likely amount to several hours of captivity. The arresting officer (in this case me) briefly explains what evidence there is to arrest the suspect (in this case Geoff) – we can't just lock people up for having a guilty-looking face now. I explain that Geoff's been naughty once more and the sergeant authorises his detention. What follows next is

20 minutes of medical questions to make sure the prisoner is safe to be detained as any deaths in police custody are seriously frowned upon by the Independent Police Complaints Commission (IPCC), and it's a big blot on the copy book of the custody sergeant too. Like any good seasoned pro, Geoff tells the sergeant he has all manner of infectious diseases, heart conditions and terminal illnesses. Fortunately the experienced custody sergeant isn't falling for any of it – but still calls a doctor to see Geoff later just in case. Next Geoff is given his custody rights which are threefold:

1. The right to have someone informed he is at the cop shop (usually via telephone)

2. The right to read a big book about codes and practices and how he has to be treated whilst in custody (not a great page turner to be honest), and...

3. The right to free and independent legal advice via a solicitor (the dark art of legal defence)

Having no friends, no desire to read a big boring book, and knowing more excuses to get him off than a whole legal firm combined, I expect Geoff to decline all three. These rights are ongoing so Geoff can change his mind at any time.

Eventually, after all his property is taken from him and recorded, it's off to a cell with Geoff, but not before he again asks in vain for another cigarette – instead having to settle for a cup of tea with five sugars.

I've no time for a tea break though; instead I'm off back to the supermarket to expeditiously gather evidence against Geoffrey. I find the security officer throwing a truant 13-year-old out of the store for eating from the pic-and-mix. He has the CCTV ready for me so we head back to the security office to watch the feature presentation.

The footage shows Geoff clearly helping himself to various items from the shelves, concealing them under his tweed, walking past the point of payment which is clearly marked, and then attempting to leave the store making no attempt to pay – a textbook 'theft from shop'. The security officers are then seen to firmly grab hold of him in a gripping up fashion before shoving him in the direction of the security office. Well what do you know? – maybe Geoff was telling me a half-truth after all. No; I quickly decide the enthusiastic security officers were just using 'reasonable force'.

Geoff's theft technique is unsubtle – to walk straight up to the items, pick them up in his grubby hands, hide them in his trend-setting apparel before trying to make a sharp exit prior to security pouncing. This is theft from shop in its crudest form, but none-the-less, this is what the police would call Geoff's 'modus operandi' (or M.O. for short). This is a Latin phrase which approximately translates as 'mode of operating'. An offender's M.O. is their preferred method of committing crime. Other villains might try to hide items within larger items and only pay for one. Some will use tools to remove security stags. Others have even been known to line bags with tin foil as they believe the stolen items will not set off security alarms if enclosed in the prepared bags. Possibly the most dismaying M.O. of all is when parents use their young children to dishonestly appropriate goods on their behalf, Fagin style! Sad but true. Geoff prefers to stick to his straightforward, no nonsense technique and – although clearly not the most successful thief – I can only assume that occasionally he gets away with it and doesn't get caught. But not today though.

Next I just need a till receipt to prove the value of the goods and a statement from the security guard. If I am lucky, the security guard will be one of the few capable of writing his own statement in a recognised format that can be evidentially used in court. Sadly though I am not lucky, and he cannot, so instead I will hand-write the statement on special police forms (an MG11 to be precise) on his behalf. The statement is fortunately fairly simple and briefly but concisely details what the security officer saw, what happened, a detailed description of the offender, and also confirms on behalf of the store that no one (especially Geoffrey Steeles) can remove stock without paying for it first. Also, for continuity reasons, Mr Security Guard must exhibit in the statement his CCTV footage and till receipt as he produced it for me: the CCTV disc and receipt are potential court exhibits and will each be given a unique reference number made up of the security guard's initials and ascending numbers for each exhibit, before being evidentially seized by me.

Good statement taking is a minor art form that must be mastered and only practice can make this perfect. *Fortunately* a rookie cop will be given countless opportunities to hone his or her statement-taking skills – trust me! Although I write out the statement, I do so from the perspective of the security officer using his words to describe the events. Once complete I ask the security officer to read my scrawlings, confirm to me it is an accurate account of the events, initial as an acknowledgement next to the numerous spelling corrections I have made, before signing in several boxes at various points on the paperwork.

It is best practice for all statements to be handwritten as it is almost impossible to be accused of doctoring them at a later date by an offender's defence solicitor. Unknowing and naive members of the public are often amazed to find out that in this modern age statements are not done on each officer's personal police issue laptop to save time and expense; I on the other hand, in this current financial climate, am just grateful we don't have to bring our own pens in from home to hand-write them.

Having all the evidence from the 'victim' I now need, and in return giving the store a crime number for their records, it's time to return to the station so Geoff can be interviewed. If I'm lucky, there will be an officer free from the Prisoner Handling Unit to take on Geoff for me and continue the interview and investigation process. Unfortunately I'm not having a particularly lucky day, and there isn't, so that chore will fall on me. I am due to finish my shift in half an hour – I will be late off.

The Geoffrey Steeles saga continues shortly so stay tuned.

8. Police Lingo

If you want to be taken seriously as a police officer, you have to learn to speak like one – *yes, yes*. Next we will talk about police language, so *stand by*, as it can be a little tricky to follow. After that I will divulge how an emergency call from a member of the public gets passed down the line and into the ear of a front-line officer via his/her personal radio – *over*. Hopefully you will *copy that* and have some understanding about how it all comes together. *By the way, those were all examples of recognised radio terminology – in case you had not guessed – out...*

The police talk funny. It's as if the public expect the cops to speak a certain way and most of the time we oblige! All police officers, myself included, feel compelled to use words and phrases that are clichéd, over-elaborate, peculiar and sometimes just downright don't really make a whole lot of sense when analysed; vocabulary that in normal conversation would never be considered appropriate, but that is just how officers are expected to converse with one another. OK, as yet I have not gone as far as to say "'Ello, 'ello, 'ello, what's going on here then?" or "Come along, let's be having you," or even "Stop in the name of the law!" But words like 'roger', 'copy', 'obliged' and 'negative' just seem to trip off the tongue naturally for inexplicable reasons. Terms that if used out of the context of the police service would most likely have the speaker labelled a jabbering, nonsensical lunatic who was in immediate need of a mental health assessment.

'Police speak' on the radio gets even more absurd. Forces use a secure and encrypted radio system called 'Airwaves' which is a mobile phone signal based network. The actual radios officers use have the appearance of large mobile handsets from the early 1990's and look like you should still be able to play the game 'Snakes' on them (sadly you can't). They are in fact very sophisticated, state of the art, highly durable, bits of kit that use GPS to track the officers location at all times. They are not walkie-talkies! These radios allow officers to be in constant communication with other officers on the ground, as well as the all knowledgeable police control room. They can even be used as regular mobile phones *and* receive simple text messages!

Another advantageous feature of the police issue radio is a little orange emergency button at the top: should a distressed officer press and hold this button for two seconds, a shrill alarm sounds in the ear of every other officer monitoring the same radio channel, causing them to drop their doughnuts and immediately rush to the aid of their comrade. Nothing summons extra police officers like a law-enforcing flash mob than that heartbeat-skipping, emergency-button sound as it is only for true priorities, when an officer in dire need has to seize the radio airwaves and interrupt any other ongoing chatter to summon assistance immediately.

TOP TIP: Below are some commonly used radio terminology and their meanings:

> **'At Scene'** – *A front-line officer will use this short phrase to confirm to the radio controller when they have arrived at an incident. Their 'time of arrival' will be noted on the computerised incident log.*

> **'Copy' or 'Received'** – *When a message has been passed, the receiver may use either phrase to confirm they have heard and understood.*

'Go ahead' – *If an officer is called, they will tell the controller this when they are listening and ready to receive a message. The controller will then transmit.*

'Out' – *This is the last word said at the end of a radio dialogue so that the other person involved knows there is nothing more to follow.*

'Read Back' – *If important information has been passed, like a vehicle registration mark, a radio operator may ask the receiver to repeat what they have just said to ensure all was received correctly.*

'Resume' – *To resume means to leave an incident and become available for another task as required.*

'Roger' – *A bit of an old fashioned expression, but still often used. This means 'understood'.*

'Stand By' – *This is used to instruct someone to wait as further information will be passed shortly.*

'Yes, Yes' – *No, I did not stutter. Because 'yes' is such a short word and can be easily missed on the radio, police officers always say it twice. 'No, no' is also used.*

Of course training will be given about how to use the radio and recognised terminology, but the best way to become fluent in 'Police Talk' is to listen to what others say. Every new recruit is terrified the first time they speak on the radio. Most have the habit of rambling on far too long for fear of not transmitting enough information, when all they really needed to say was "Area search, no trace" (translated as "had a look, but couldn't find anything") for example. Radio speech is another skill that mostly comes with experience and practice. A good radio transmission is one that includes all the relevant information you are trying to convey, but in the shortest number of words possible, which can be summarised with the following 'ABC' acronym straight out of training school:

Accuracy, Brevity, Clarity

Only one person at a time can talk on the radio and there is nothing more frustrating than when you have an urgent update to pass to Control Room but you can't because a PCSO the other side of the county is rambling on about nuisance youths playing football on a patch of grass clearly marked 'No Ball Games'. Often when the PCSO is finished prattling on about the heinous crime they've just witnessed, all the other officers waiting to transmit something they deem relevant will frantically try to time pressing their radio transmit button a thousandths of a second after the PCSO has released his. The lucky winner gets the air and can talk to the operator, whilst the losers are condemned to having to wait once more for their turn to come and hoping for better luck next time.

Calling All Cars, Calling All Cars

Below is an example of a radio dialogue, using real police terms, but set in the context of an everyday domestic situation for simplicity – as well as humorous effect.

Dad (call sign Delta 1): *Delta 1 to Mike 1, are you receiving, over?*

Mum (call sign Mike 1): *Mike 1 receiving loud and clear, go ahead, over.*

Delta 1: *When convenient, please can a free unit convey the condiments to me, over?*

Mike 1: *Delta 1, confirm, salt, pepper and ketchup?*

Delta 1: *That's a yes, yes, over.*

Mike 1: *Stand by, I'll see if I have a unit available. Tango 1 are you monitoring this channel, over?*

Silence...

Mike 1: *Mike 1 to Tango 1, are you monitoring this radio channel?*

Long pause

Mike 1: I repeat, *Mike 1 to Tango 1, are you receiving? Over!*

Little Timmy (call sign Tango 1): *huh ... Tango 1, to Mike 1, are you calling me?*

Mike 1: *Yes, yes.*

Tango 1: *Apologies, radio signal is not good, now receiving loud and cl... zzzzz... click... beep...* [The Airwaves radio system coverage is by no means perfect.]

Mike 1: *Tango 1 your transmission was broken. Are you available for a quick dispatch job? We require sauces dropping off, would you be able to oblige, over?*

Tango 1: *Tango 1 received, Mike 1 what's the response grading level on that job, and who's the informant please?*

Mike 1: *It's on as a 'priority' job, and your dad has called it in, over.*

Tango 1: *Yes, yes. All received. On route.*

87

A few minutes later...

Tango 1: *At scene.*

Mike 1: *Copy.*

Tango 1: *Tango 1 to Mike 1, over.*

Mike 1: *Go ahead.*

Tango 1: *I have custody of the salt and pepper but I'm unable to reach the ketchup. I have eyeball on the ketchup. Can another unit back up, over?*

Mike 1: *Stand by ...Tango 2, receiving?*

Little Tamara (call sign Tango 2): *Tango 2 receiving, go ahead.*

Mike 1: *Tango 2, what's you location and status* [availability for a job], *over?*

Tango 2: *At the dinner table and available if required, but I'm off duty in half an hour, over.*

Mike 1: *You're the only unit as showing on duty. Did you copy the last from Tango 1?*

Tango 2: *Yes, yes, roger that. If there is no one else show me backing up. ETA 1 minute.*

A short delay later

Tango 2: *Tango 2 calling Mike 1*

Mike 1: *Go ahead, Tango 2*

Tango 2: *Show me at scene please. I am RV* [rendezvous] *with Tango 1.*

Finally...

Tango 1: *Tango 1 to Mike 1, over*

Mike 1: *Go ahead*

Tango 1: *Delta 1 is in receipt of the package. Please update the log and then that job can be closed. I am now resuming. Out.*

In the above example, like in any household, Mum is the controller. Each unit is given a unique call sign. This might be the officer's collar number (sometimes called warrant number. This is the unique identification number each officer is issued when starting the job and will most likely be known by it for the rest of their career), or a specific combination of letters and numbers that relate to that type of officer and their home station. Specialist units like firearms, dogs or traffic will have unique call signs to differentiate themselves from other unit types like front-line divisional officers. A dog unit for example might have the prefix 'delta' at the start of his/her call sign, whereas traffic might start with 'tango'. Each force will be different but the system used should (in theory at least) make distinguishing between different officer types a simpler task for other units, as well as radio controllers who dish out the emergency calls.

I'll take this opportunity to explain how a 999 call from the public gets put out to a response officer on the radio. It's a bit like a grand game of Chinese whispers and there are four players involved.

1. The Informant

Not a paid supplier of information on the mafia – the informant is in fact a member of the public who calls the police to report a crime or incident. They may be the victim – or 'injured party' (IP to use the police term) – or a helpful witness. Alternatively they might be a drunk numpty with too much time on their hands and a penchant for wasting police time!

2. *The Call Handler*

A civilian call handler employed by the force will pick up the phone and listen to the informant. They will immediately generate a computerised incident log. All calls to the police are recorded but in the log the call handler will type details about the informant – their name, address, phone number – then summarise what they are saying and what service they want from their dutiful police force in exchange for their taxes. This can be anything from immediate assistance as their husband is trying to break through the bathroom door to kill them, to a taxi ride home as they have spent all their hard-earned benefits on alcohol by mistake (again). The latter are told where to go, whilst the former are given advice on making barricades before police can arrive. Once a log is created and updated the incident is quickly given a response grading. This means it is prioritised as to how promptly police officers need to attend. Usually there are four options here:

> *Telephone Resolution* – "Someone's stolen my snowman", "Terminator 3 is a terrible sequel and is causing me great harassment, alarm and distress being on ITV right now", "I've just seen a suspicious looking squirrel on Buttercup Avenue," are all examples of inappropriate 999 calls the police regularly receive. The informant is either patronisingly thanked for their call, or warned it's a criminal offence to misuse the 999 number, before the call is terminated.

If it is a sincere and genuine call, but can be dealt with by helpful advice over the phone without the need for police attendance, it would also fall in this category.

Routine – Trivial matters that officers will need to look into but won't be busting a gut to get there. This might be an unwitnessed criminal damage that occurred an unknown time ago, or inconsiderate parking issues that local/neighbourhood teams will sort out when they get round to it. These jobs will form an orderly queue and be dealt with when an officer is available and not much else is going on so that the job can be 'resourced' (have an officer sent out).

Priority/Prompt – Usually these have an associated timescale of 15 to 30 minutes (depending on the force in question) in which time officers will aim to attend. These are jobs that need the police there sooner rather than later but most probably do not justify a blue light run. Force policies usually dictate that domestic incidents where the vulnerable party is safe and at no risk will still be graded as a 'priority'. Burglaries will also fall into this category as, for the reassurance of the victim, officers will attend promptly. Some road traffic collisions will be deemed worthy of a 'priority response' as infrastructures need to be kept open at all times, as an obstructed highway for only a short period of time can still cause untold misery to many.

Immediate/Urgent/Emergency – Often accompanied by an hysterical drunkard shouting in the background of the call ("Get the rozzers here quick, it's all kicking off!") this a chance for a response officer to bring the noise (siren) and go charging across town on an adrenaline-fuelled blue-light run. This is the reason many young officers sign up. Anything from violent domestics, fights, burglaries in progress, to serious traffic accidents fall into this tier. Usually an officer is guaranteed one of two things when his/her car comes to a tyre-smoking, screeching halt, half up a pavement – a baddy to chase and/or arrest, or copious amounts of paperwork!

3. Radio Controller/Dispatcher

Once a log has been created and optimistically all the relevant and required facts have been acquired, the information is electronically pinged over to the radio controller. These have to be particularly switched on individuals who will have a headset on and several computer screens at their disposal. Their responsibility is knowing where 'resources' (officers) are and what their availability is so that they can then dispatch those available officers to the jobs as they come in. Resource juggling is a tricky and unenviable task; unsurprisingly there are never enough officers when the proverbial fan gets hit. Some radio controllers are civilians, some sworn police officers. Some are very good at their job and remain calm and accomplished throughout no matter what chaos is going on in the streets; some are so annoying and frustrating they make you want to drive straight to the control room and inflict all sorts of physical atrocities on them (but you mustn't). Regardless, it's always advisable to stay in the radio controller's good book, as they decide which officer gets dispatched to the report of a naked fat man who has fallen off the toilet and now can't get up, or who gets to chase escaped sheep around the road in the pouring rain etc. Think carefully before making flippant remarks on the radio as in my experience radio controllers have long memories, so be warned!

4. Response Officer

Well that's me – and maybe you, one day. Using the GPS capabilities of the officer's radio, the controller will direct in the closest ground unit to the location in which they are required. Officers converse with the radio controller to obtain details about what has happened as well as any background information that can be extracted from police systems to benefit the officer before he/she arrives at the potential war zone. If an officer wants to know something else from the original informant he/she will ask the radio controller, who will ask the call handler, who in turn will ask the informant. The information then gets passed back along the line until it eventually reaches the enquiring officer several frustrating moments later.

This whole process only takes a matter of minutes, but even a short delay can be the difference between getting to a location on time or not.

FACT: The 999 emergency number was introduced in the London area on 30th June 1937. Glasgow followed a year later and other cities after the war, but the service did not become available to all the UK until 1976. In 2011, 37 million 999 calls were made and 98% were answered within 5 seconds; 52% of those were connected to the police, 41% the ambulance service, 6% to the fire service and 1% to the coastguard/cave and mountain rescue. Source: BT, Cable & Wireless.

9. Mental Health, Missing People, and Mad Mary

Mental health and missing persons don't always go hand in hand; often missing people are just rebellious children, high on E numbers, who've run away for a few hours because mum's taken away their PS3 or Xbox after they refused to do maths homework. Sometimes we find them down the park with their mates and a 2-litre bottle of cider; sometimes we haven't a clue where they are but nevertheless they return home, safe and sound, of their own accord when it gets cold and dark and they miss satellite TV. Fortunately it's very rare that, one way or another, the delinquent isn't returned home to a furious parent with a serious grounding inevitable. Often we find ourselves hunting the same serial missing persons (or Misper, to use the abbreviated police terminology) on an almost weekly basis. As children find their place in the world, some try to push boundaries and test the limits of their parents, Social Services and of course the increasingly shortening arm of the law.

Once the child is located hiding out at their friend's house, the juvenile and police officer usually enter into a frustrating negotiation as to under what circumstances offspring and parent are to be reunited. The insubordinate young person will seldom return home without a fight as their parents are of course the worst in the world and life under their rent-free roof is "so unfair!"

If it's a stroppy teenager who has for the first time 'done a runner', often a cunning officer can bluff them into returning home by creating a mythical law that states, when found, children have to retreat back to their original dwelling – Section 1 of the Hide and Seek

Act of 2008. The problem comes when the young person regularly goes A.W.O.L. and knows the stark reality that police have no power to return children home unless said child is at risk remaining where they are, or a court order of some sort is in place. Adolescent teenagers can be very stubborn and will test an officer's resolve to the limits.

FACT: A study found that every year 84,000 under 16-year-olds run away overnight on at least one occasion in England. However only 17% of runaways in that study were reported to the police. Source: The Children's Society.

Unlike in American films, a person does not have to be missing for 24 hours before the police will start looking. The proficient police officer's duties at a missing person incident involves collating relevant information about the missing individual from the person reporting them missing. This information is straightforward stuff like getting a good description, finding out where and when they were last seen and where they are likely to go so we can start looking. Other important information would be when they had their last meal, if they have access to transport, if they possess any cash, and if there are any medical conditions apparent and/or medication required.

There will also be a necessity for officers to conduct a thorough search of the Misper's home. This is for any notes or clues that might suggest where the Misper has absconded to and if they have made preparations to leave – like personal belongings taken, cash or clothes removed, etc. – but constables are also searching for any more sinister clues that might explain a disappearance – signs of a struggle, blood, the Misper's severed head in the freezer, etc. Finally try to obtain a recent photo and the Misper's toothbrush or hairbrush. The latter items are in case we have to obtain their DNA to determine forensically where the Misper's been or to confirm the identity of decomposing remains dredged from the bottom of a river several weeks in the future. (Probably best not to reveal that bit to an already distressed and emotional parent just yet though!)

Once all the information is acquired a supervisor will decide if the Misper is low, medium or high risk:

Low Risk: The person reporting does not know the whereabouts of the Misper, but there is nothing to suggest the Misper is vulnerable or in any danger. This is usually an adult that needs a bit of time to themselves, and in all honesty the police won't be doing a whole lot to find them. After all, just because a person doesn't know where their partner is, it doesn't necessarily make them missing.

Medium Risk: The police would like to find this person sooner rather than later so will carry out address checks at friends and family, make enquiries with hospitals and also other police force's custodies – in case they've been arrested! This might be a person who regularly goes missing or someone with mild mental health issues and/or depression, but there is nothing to suggest imminent harm will come to them.

High Risk: You're getting off duty late. Ring your partner and let them know. Dinner will be in the dog *again* by the time you get home! This is a person who *is* at imminent risk of harm and is certainly vulnerable. Examples would be young children, mental health and/or disability sufferers unable to interact with the public on their own, people who present a risk to themselves and/or the public and those deemed suicidal. In this instance, officers will be asked to flood any area the Misper is likely to be and a police helicopter and dog units are likely to be deployed if there is scope for them.

In extreme cases of life and death, senior officers may decide to 'ping' a Misper's mobile telephone. If switched on a signal can be sent to the phone. When the phone receives that signal the location can be triangulated between mobile phone cell sites (aerials) and an approximate vicinity can be established. The more local cell sites near to the phone, the more accurate the result – so large, built-up towns are good, but sparse woody areas are tricky. This is called 'cell site analysis' and is an incredibly powerful tool. Sadly, it is only at police disposal in extreme, potentially fatal circumstances as anything else would be deemed an invasion of an individual's privacy.

Hide and Seek

Trying to track down missing teenagers can be a good game – a bit like a hormone-inspired treasure hunt if you will:

15-year-old Kieran Jones is missing so, as his distraught mum suggests, I might go and see his best mate Luke first...

"I ain't seen him for ages, not since he stole my girlfriend Holly off me. I'm gonna punch him if I do see him!" states a jilted Luke.

Not much assistance is forthcoming here so I go and

see that young jezebel Holly...

"Why would I be with that ****er!? Not after he dumped me for that Samantha Trollchild," declares a jealous Holly. "But I ain't even bovvered coz he was a rubbish kisser! And anywayz, I heard it was only coz she lets boys touch her boobs for 50p!"

So next stop is the Trollchild residence...

"Whatever! I wouldn't tell you even if I did know where he woz, copper! Yous probably just wants to arrest him anyway, blood!" announces a grammatically challenged Samantha.

You get the idea.

The problem with this sort of missing person is that they usually don't want to be found; but sometimes the most worrying missing people are those that do not even realise they're missing. People with mental health issues are everywhere. As a regular member of the public, you spend your time endeavouring to avoid the weird-looking tramp trying to catch and bite the heads off live pigeons in the town square; but as a police officer you spend a large proportion of your time actively seeking out these people and enticing them into your patrol car.

Meet 'Mad' Mary MacDonald. Aged in her late 40's, she is a white female of plump build, with short, curly, mousey hair and wears glasses. She lives on her own since her grown up son moved out. Her house is clean and well kept. She once told me she used to work in a bank before she became mentally ill. Apart from the bright red lipstick she always applies to her face in a clown like fashion, Mary appears to be a normal, upstanding member of society. Often mental health problems are self-inflicted – brought on by years of alcohol or substance abuse – but not in Mary's case. As you'll learn from your training, mental health is a non-discriminatory disease that can affect anyone from any background, at any time.

Mary's sanity varies from that which is easily comparable to the standard of many of my colleagues (so almost normal), to the other end of the scale which finds her running around the town centre, half naked, with a roast chicken on her head. It was the latter episode that landed her inside Sunrise House, an NHS secure unit for mental health suffers.

Now 'secure' is a rather ambiguous term in this context. The unit certainly is secure, but only if the inmates are incapable of walking up to an often unattended automatic electric door and then taking a bold step outside.

POWER: Section 136 of the Mental Health Act gives the police the authority to remove a person from a public place to a 'place of safety', either for their own protection or for the protection of others, so that their immediate needs can be properly assessed. The place of safety is usually a hospital or specialist centre for mental health patients. Once there, a doctor, approved mental health professional and/or social worker will meet with and examine the detainee to decide how best to help them.

It's 6 p.m. as I patrol the streets. I have a crewmate today: his name is Special Constable Dominic Fakename. A 19-year-old who seems a nice lad, if a little green and naive. He works in Halfords during the week (although I'm sure he tells people, especially girls, he's actually a full-time law man) but one day aspirers to be a real cop just as soon as he's gained some 'life experience'. Between you and me, if I am honest, I don't think he is cut out for it and will never get past the assessment centre, but at least I've got a companion to talk to for the next 10 hours and, if we get into a scrap with someone, he also presents a viable alternative target for them, so I'm not complaining. The Special Constabulary are a group of brave individuals who have the same police powers as a regular officer like me. However, unlike me, they do not get paid to protect and serve – they work any hours they can spare as a volunteer.

TOP TIP: If you have the free time and inclination, being a special constable is a great way to experience the police service before deciding if it's the right career choice for you. In fact many forces will now only consider applicants for full time police officer positions who have previously served time in the Special Constabulary or as a PCSO. Training is provided over a series of weekends and when complete, 'specials' work alongside and support full-time regular officers. Expenses are paid and officers are asked to give up a minimum of 16 hours of their spare time a month. If your chosen force is not recruiting full-time officers at present, this might be a worthwhile alternative. Make enquiries with the recruitment team.

"...so once I've fitted the new exhaust, my baby should have an extra five- to ten-brake horsepower and will sound so cool!"

"That's nice, Dom."

Just as Dominic is starting to bore me with a story about the latest modifications he's planning to make to his Vauxhall Corsa Sri, the radio timely interrupts and we're asked by control room to attend Sunrise House, as a guest has once again gone walkabout. No other details are forthcoming from the radio handler so young Dom and I make our way to find out what has happened.

As we walk (unchallenged I might add) into the reception area, a plump, black male in his mid-30's waddles up to us with a broad smile on his face. For a brief moment I'm playing 'doctor/patient roulette' as I have no idea which one he is. Even the lanyard with an ID attached around his neck isn't a conclusive certainty.

"Are you here about Mary? She's missing again," he says.

I'll give him the benefit of the doubt: doctor.

"We are. Can we sit down and take a few details?" I suggest.

Some would be astonished that the staff have no idea when exactly she left, what she had with her, or even what she was wearing, but this does not surprise me at all. All they can tell me is that it was sometime in the last three hours, she isn't likely to be armed and dangerous, it is probable she is clothed although we do not know in what, and on this occasion it is highly unlikely she is in possession of any poultry products. I'm not at all astounded at the lack of assistance the staff can give as I have been here many times before and know this is the norm. In fact I'm grateful she only has a three-hour head start over us.

I update control room with all that I haven't found out at the NHS insecure unit. The radio handler passes a vague description of Mary and the circumstances under which she's gone missing to the other officers on duty so they can keep an eye out during their patrols. This type of radio announcement is called an 'attention to' as officers are asked to pay attention to something (that's police logic).

Just as Dom and I climb into our car a PCSO in the town centre team calls up on the radio. Over the air, he broadcasts he has been stopped by a man walking his dog who has seen a confused white woman wearing a pink dressing gown sitting on the old abandoned railway bridge over London Road. He goes on to say that apparently the woman is carrying a roast chicken under her arm. Now I'm no detective, but I know who that might be...

Once again it is time to fire up all 90-brake horsepower of our Astra diesel to fly to Mary's rescue.

"You know, they could get so much more power out of these pandas if they uprated the ECUs, improved the induction and boosted the turbo pressure."

"That's nice, Dom."

With blue LED lights strobing and sirens blaring we're heading to London Road as quickly as traffic allows. Mary is indeed sat atop the bridge with her slippers dangling perilously close to lorries passing under her. Unnervingly the dressing gown belt is round her neck. Like an ominous, symbolic premonition of the future, the roast chicken is laying squashed on the tarmac below.

Other units are hurtling to assist us but we are first on scene. We approach with lights and sirens now off so as not to startle Mary and cause her to join the chicken beneath. I park a safe distance away before passing an update via my radio of what I can see.

Whilst Dom attempts to stop traffic, narrowly avoiding becoming a pedestrian road death statistic as he does so, I walk under Mary to engage her in conversation. Response officers are not trained negotiators; in fact I do not recall any of my comprehensive training being relevant in these circumstances.

Having now located the not-so-elusive Mary, she is no longer a missing person. She has evolved into what the police officially call a 'Concern For Safety'. If this story doesn't have a happy ending she might very well turn into what the police officially call a 'Sudden Death'. In this event I will be in a great big, steaming pile of what the police *un*officially call 'Deep Sh...', well, I'm sure you know what I mean.

As I open my mouth for the first time no words come out so I take a few extra seconds to compose myself and decide the best approach to start a dialogue with Mary. My opening gambit was probably far too blunt for the occasion but, not really having a clue what else to say, seemed acceptable:

"Mary, what the hell are you doing?!"

"Randolph?"

Wow. That's a response I wasn't expecting. I've no idea who Randolph is – but it's most likely neither does Mary. She might think I'm Randy the Yorkshire terrier she had during her childhood for all I know, as her state of mind seems somewhat disturbed right now. I just hope Randolph is not the squished chicken on the road below her.

"No Mary, it's PC Surname. The police. I'm here to help. Tell me how I can help."

I've met Mary on several occasions but I don't think I have made enough of an impression for her to recognise or remember me.

Members of the public are now gathering on the pavement staring at Mary and me. Some are smiling and evidently enjoying the show. It seems Mary has scaled a fence and clambered up a bank of dirt to reach her perch. I make a move to do the same but Mary screams at me not to come up or she'll jump.

Instead, continuing with my blunt, direct and most likely improper line of questioning, I shout up to Mary again:

"What are you doing?"

"He says I've got to jump," she replies.

"Who does?" I ask, a little baffled.

"Satan! Who do you think?!"

Ah, of course, I now remember that last time we spoke just a few weeks ago, Mary was on first name terms with the dark lord himself and told me she regularly chatted with him.

The watching crowd must number 50 or so now, as even more start to spill out of an overlooking pub.

I'm certainly not panicking, but would definitely admit I'm a little flummoxed as to how best proceed and bring this to a positive outcome.

"You don't wanna listen to what he says. He's no good!" I yell up, waving my hand in as dismissive gesture to emphasise the point as I vainly attempt to point out that the Devil may not be the best confidant for her.

"Do you want to talk to him?" she suggests.

Tempting. But no, not right now. "No thanks. I'd rather talk to you. Tell Satan you're not doing it, Mary."

"He says he wants to talk to you," Mary insists.

"I can't talk to Satan right now, Mary. It's not a good time."

"He says it's important," Mary continues.

"I really can't chat with him now, sorry."

"Shall I take a message for you then?"

"Erm, OK. Thanks." I look forward to hearing my message later."

I know to acquiesce with Mary's fantasies probably is not beneficial to her long-term treatment and recovery, but all I am interested in right now is avoiding her skull shattering on the tarmac below. The fall might not kill her outright, but still isn't going to do her any favours.

Perhaps unsurprisingly, pointing out to Mary that the Devil might be a negative influence does not seem to have had the desired effect and altered her intentions. She turns to her right and converses with an invisible Satan as I awkwardly look up. I can barely hear one side of the conversation as Mary mumbles away to herself, but it appears Satan is quite convincing, as she nods away at him in apparent agreement with his sinister suggestions. She turns back to me.

"Randolph?! Don't come any closer. He says I've gotta jump and kill myself," she states as she rises to her feet, along with the tension and my blood pressure.

Gasps can be heard from the watching spectators.

There seems little point in explaining Randolph is not familiar to me, so instead I say, "Think of all the people who love you. They don't want you to do it. Erm … Randolph would miss you. Besides, it's the weekend tomorrow!" I'm clutching at straws a bit now.

"I've got no plans," is the rebuff. "Is Randolph with you?"

"Erm… not right now, Mary. Where is Randolph, maybe I can get him for you?"

"Last I heard he was in Broadmoor doing a 7-year stretch."

Oh dear.

"Erm… OK, I'll see what I can do, Mary."

"Randolph!? Is that you?"

"No, Mary. It's still me, PC Surname, remember?"

"Where's Randolph, is he with you?"

I fear we may be going around in circles here.

It's at this moment, as I gaze up at Mary, I notice just over her left shoulder and approximately 200,000 miles behind her a possible explanation for her peculiar behaviour: there is a full moon tonight. Although there is probably very little scientific evidence to support it, if you ask any copper they will confirm that nights with full moons are always the busiest!

As I struggle to control the escalating situation and more emergency services arrive at the scene, the radio controller is constantly asking for updates from me via my earpiece. I'm reluctant to answer as I do not know if it would be ideal for Mary to know I'm also hearing voices in my head. Really my crewmate Dom, who's now standing next to me, should be passing information to the control room on my behalf, but by the shocked look on his inexperienced face, he is more bamboozled than I am.

As Mary again continues to chat with the Dark Prince, I take the opportunity to tilt my head to my radio and whisper an update. I'm told that a negotiator is on the way – with an ETA of 45 minutes! Trained police negotiators are sparse and mostly likely an off-duty one has been disturbed from his dinner and asked to attend the scene. (He will also be on overtime so they are therefore expensive too.)

After this most recent pep talk from her evil advisor, Mary has a more anxious look on her face as she turns back to the two police officers below. She leans forward, teetering on the concrete edge, gazing at the bewildered officers. The on looking crowd gasps again but some continue to film the action on their iPhones. I truly hope Mary isn't about to become an Internet sensation on YouTube. Up until now it had not actually fully occurred to me that she might really do it; coaxing people out of doing something silly is a fairly common occurrence for police officers. Granted, it is usually not matters of life and death; instead instances such as persuading people to open doors, or hand back their soon to be ex partner's car keys that they just removed and fled the house with.

But now it's dawned on me she really could do it. What do I do if she does? Should I try and catch her? What happens if you try to catch a 13-stone woman falling on your head from 25ft up? Am I likely to receive a commendation if my spine does indeed break her fall and my back along with it? Would it be better for all if she fell on Dom instead?

Now rising up on to her tiptoes its looks inevitable what is going to happen. This is it, Mary's going to fly! The group of gawping teenagers with smart phones in hand smile gleefully in anticipation at the pending finale to Mary's spectacular performance. But suddenly a squeaky little voice just behind me cuts the tension:

"Mary, can you come down please?"

It was Dom. Bless him, he's having a go. It was worth a try.

But hang on – to my astonishment Mary's gaze is drawn to my special constable friend. A calmness sweeps across her face. Mary sinks back on her heels and takes a step back from the brink.

"Ok Randolph, if you say so."

Dom and I stare at each other in amazement as she appears to walk back to the side of the bridge, and ungracefully stumbles down the slope. The group of ogling teenagers sigh with disappointment a few yards away and start to make their way back to their southern fried chicken hangout. Without a fuss Mary allows me to escort her to an awaiting ambulance with accompanying paramedics who will check her over.

My sergeant has now arrived and joins me at the rear of the ambulance as Mary is seen to.

"Good work, lads," says the sarge.

"No probs, Boss," I reply. "All in a day's work." Still incredibly bemused as to how this episode was brought to a successful conclusion.

"Mary, are you ok? No injuries?" Sarge checks.

"No! You must be joking! I wouldn't do anything silly," Mary announces now with a deliriously happy smile on her face.

The turnaround in Mary's demeanour is nothing short of spectacular.

"Are you going to go back to the hospital so they can check you over please, Mary?" continues my supervisor.

"That sounds like a lovely idea, Officer. I like it at the hospital."

"Why did you not come down sooner then, Dear?" the sergeant quizzes her.

"Well they didn't ask me to!" Mary explains.

"Pardon, Mary?"

"Well no one asked me to come down."

"You mean you didn't come down before because the officers didn't ask you to?" enquires my supervisor, his voice growing with a mixture of confusion and anger in equal measure.

The sergeant turns to me with eyebrows raised. "Surname, is this true?"

I can see the rest of my shift – who have by now all arrived – smirking at me over the sergeant's shoulder. They're laughing at me as if watching a naughty schoolmate who is about to have the head teacher explode at them.

"Well ... of course I ... but ... she ..."

I rack my mind for an answer. Surely I would have asked her to come down? Maybe not. Instead, resigning myself to the truth: "No, Sarge, I guess I didn't," I reply with a tone of self-disappointment.

"I did though, Sarge!" Dom, standing next to me, smugly betrays me.

"Yeah, he's a good lad that one. A credit to the uniform. You could learn a lot from him," chirps up Mary with an unhelpful suggestion and only compounding my embarrassment further.

"Good work, Fakename! You'll get a commendation for this," before sternly adding, "Surname, we'll discuss this later."

I'm dumbfounded for a few seconds as to what has just happened, but then reality hits me. Fair play to Dom, he's the unlikely hero on this occasion – the day belongs to him. I always said that boy will make chief superintendent one day.

I know that I'll be teased for this for many months to come by my colleagues at the station when word of this inevitably gets out. The ribbing will only cease when someone else on the team makes the next foolish mistake of note. Before I slope back to station to prepare for the banter to begin, there's one thing I have to know: "Mary, who *is* Randolph?"

She screws her face up in disdain and bewilderment at me. "Who?! No idea. Don't know what you're talking about. You're as crazy as a box of frogs, mate!" is the last thing she says before the ambulance doors close and she is whisked back to the semi-security of Sunrise House.

10. Priority Crime: the Facts and Figures

Burglaries and robberies are a contentious issue for all 43 forces. They are deemed priority crimes because, although the financial loss might be smaller when compared to other crimes like frauds and commercial burglaries, the personal impact they have on the victim is great: understandably no-one likes to know that whilst they were out at their daughters school play, a stranger was rifling through their underwear drawer in search of the family's life savings, but instead settling for their grandfather's war medals. Likewise not many enjoy being threatened at knife point whilst being forced to hand over their iPhone, mountain bike and new Converse All-Star trainers as it's a long walk home.

Being priority crimes, the government rightly places great emphasis on their detection and reduction, and the motivational national performance tables (mentioned later on) reflect this: if burglaries and robberies are up in a force area, then that constabulary will be down when the latest league table of best performing forces is issued.

Although police forces can impact upon the volume of such crimes by endeavouring to lock up their most prolific burglars and robbers, there is always a steady stream of up-and-coming young scroats to take their places. The battle is never ending which causes great frustration and consternation to the bigwigs at HQ about how best to combat this scourge. There are however a couple of options.

Option One

The force with the burglary epidemic could set up a specific task force who will devise a special operation with a cool and dynamic sounding name like 'Operation Strike Back' to tackle the problem head-on. They could mobilize the PCSOs to do leaflet drops throughout the theft-ravaged estates, warning the citizens to be extra vigilant and lock their doors. Perhaps a local newspaper and radio campaign could be utilised to publicise ways residents can do their bit and protect their own homes against theft. Whilst extra-high visibility policing around the clock and undercover officers on overtime in plain clothes covertly patrolling around the worst hit neighbourhoods – getting in the faces of the known offenders so they recognise that under no uncertain terms will their burgling ways be tolerated – will almost certainly drive down the crime rates! *But* that sounds like a very time-consuming and expensive solution. Maybe there is another way...

Option Two

Alternatively, a much easier and cost effective way to reduce the number of reported burglaries and robberies is to simply deny they are happening – that way the Home Office will never know! This might sound a little wacky, but let me explain in a semi-algebraic form (as after all, basic maths skill is an essential police requirement).

X = *very bad*
Y = *still bad, but Y < X*

$$robbery = X, however...$$

('assault') + ('theft' from slightly dazed person) = Y, they'll be OK

Likewise:

('attempt burglary') = X, however...

('criminal damage' to back window caused by screwdriver) + (no witnesses) = Y, small crime and no real need for further investigation.

(A bona fide 'burglary') + (unhappy homeowner) = big fat X,

but...

(A 'theft in a dwelling' as offender might be known to the victim and therefore not a trespasser) + (disgruntled victim) = Y: not ideal but still much more acceptable

Conclusion: believe it or not, it's actually better to record two 'smaller' crimes rather than one big, fat robbery or burglary that'll only scare the Home Office as well as the locals, right?!

By creatively categorising reported crimes and effectively 'massaging figures', forces can make spectacular improvements to their performance overall, whilst actually spending less money as they're not having to bother with as much of that expensive 'proactive policing' and 'investigation' stuff! Although the ethics of this practice is highly dubious, it is now commonplace throughout the UK and will be wholly supported by any government as this propaganda all helps come election time when crime appears down, the streets seem safer and the "tide is turning in the war on crime".

FACT: An international study found that England and Wales had more burglaries and robberies per 100,000 people than the USA. Source: study by UN Office on Drugs and Crime published in 2010.

Where's the Telly Gone?!

A 'burglary dwelling' is a theft that occurs in a place where a person lives. Usually small electrical items, cash and jewellery are the target. For it to qualify as a burglary, the offender must have entered as a trespasser, meaning they had no lawful reason to be in that house. It does not matter if entry was forced or the premises left insecure by mistake (although the victim's insurance company may have something to say if it is a case of the latter). Any burglary which occurs somewhere other than a dwelling is referred to as a 'burglary other' (such as in a warehouse or office) and – although still a crime and serious matter – will not be given as much precedence as the 'house' variety.

The majority of cars stolen nowadays are done so during a burglary. As vehicle security has improved significantly in recent time, stealing cars has become a sterner task; no longer can a petty crook just pop open a door with a bent coat hanger, pull a few wires from under the steering wheel, make a couple of sparks and be *Gone In Sixty Seconds* – contrary to Nicholas Cage and Hollywood. By far the easiest thing to do is find the car you fancy on a driveway, break in to the house, help yourself to the keys (and their Xbox whilst you're at it) and disappear into the night before the Feds arrive. Once you have your new ride, simply screw on the number plates freshly stolen from another car – preferably of the same make, model and colour as the one just acquired – and you're all set.

High performance and rare cars are often specifically targeted via burglaries either to have their identifying chassis and engine numbers changed, or for immediate export to foreign fields.

Fact: A study of 9,000 vehicle thefts recorded on the Police National Computer found that 50.6% of those occurred when the vehicle was left at the owner's home address or nearby. Source: ACPO Vehicle Crime Intelligence Service 2011.

In most cases a burglary is discovered by a distraught homeowner returning to find their once pristine house upside down, before reporting it to the police. A front-line officer will generally be the first to attend the scene. Conducting house-to-house enquiries with neighbours and potential witnesses is a routine primary investigation. Giving advice to the victim about preservation of the scene for forensic examination is of the utmost importance as any evidence this generates is usually the downfall of the burglars. Ideally the house should remain as 'sterile' (or untouched) as possible until scenes of crime officers can attend and do their bit. Most forces do not have 24-hour SOCO officers so it may be the case that they cannot attend until the morning.

Invariably burglaries are some of the most frustrating crimes for officers to attend as there is often little that can be done there and then to comfort the distressed victim. The suspects are usually long gone hours before and the likelihood of recovering any property is practically zero as the criminal will quickly sell on the goods to a 'handler' or 'fence' (someone without scruples who will knowingly buy stolen goods).

Often the perpetrators of burglaries are drug addicts having an addiction to support and as such will prolifically commit burglaries to fund their habit. When a burglar (or robber, which follows) is finally caught the police have powers to search their vehicles, home addresses and the associated addresses of the person in custody. Although stolen goods are moved on hastily, when executing these search warrants, officers have the opportunity to seize items in the possession of the accused that are suspected to be stolen, as well as gather other clues and forensic evidence to further the investigation (e.g. clothing, footwear, mobile phones, financial documentation, etc.), and even link the suspect to other offences.

*POWER: When a person has been arrested, Section 32 of the Police And Criminal Evidence Act (PACE) 1984 allows a police officer to search any premises in which the arrest took place, or any premises which the prisoner was in immediately prior to arrest. The searching officers are looking for any similar items in connection with the arrested offence, **however** any other criminal items found will also be seized and the detainee further arrested if applicable.*

POWER: A Section 18 of PACE 1984 search warrant permits a constable to enter a premise (by force if required) occupied or controlled by a person already under arrest and at a police station. In order for such a warrant to be issued by a senior officer there must be reasonable grounds to suspect similar items in connection with the offence arrested for will be found at the address. Again any other unconnected but still criminal items found will be seized and dealt with accordingly.

Stick 'Em Up, This is a Robbery

A robbery involves a theft whereby the victim was *deliberately* put in fear that force would be used – or indeed was used – in order to steal. Robberies are where the greatest creative license is used with regards to crime figures: did the suspect just ninja kick a random member of the public (an assault) and then, whilst still with the victim, spontaneously decide to casually help themselves to the contents of the victims pockets (a 'theft from person' offence) therefore committing two separate crimes but definitely not a robbery? Believe it or not, from a crime severity and recording point of view it is much better if they did, rather than the police being able to conclusively prove that committing theft using fear was the intention of the villain from the outset! Welcome to the crazy world of police statistics! Honest, hard-working front-line constables would much prefer the genuine crime is recorded – after all it makes no difference to them so why not be honest? – but increasing pressure from the powers above have influence over a force's behaviour and discretion.

A weapon does not have to be involved during a robbery, but in many cases is. The increasing use of weapons on today's streets is well publicised in the media. Despite this the UK actually has some of the strictest laws in the world governing the distribution and possession of knives and guns in particular (although most officers would argue sufficient sentencing guidance is often still lacking). If reports are that armed suspects are likely to still be at a location or in a certain area where a crime has just occurred, front-line police officers will be dispatched with the backup and support of specialist units with extra training and protection, such as armed response units (ARUs or firearms officers), dog units, PSU/TSG vans (discussed later) and/or traffic officers. Use of the police helicopter may also be considered as 'the eye in the sky' can be invaluable in locating and containing suspects. Front-line divisional units may be instructed to attend the locality for 'sightings only', meaning they are not to directly engage any armed and dangerous suspects/subjects, and instead alert their control room of any sightings whilst remaining in the relative safety of their patrol vehicles. In reality if a divisional officer does stumble across a suspect, irrespective of them being 'tooled up' or not, the temptation is often to attempt to apprehend, as just driving by and potentially letting a suspect flee is not in most police officer's nature. However personal safety should be paramount to any officer as this is only a job after all.

Robberies range from the very common and simple 'schoolyard' type thefts of BMXs, up to the thankfully rarer armed varieties at banks, bookmakers, off-licenses and any other store. Just like with any crime, an 'attempted' robbery is treated as seriously as a successful one – and hopefully punished equally too. Obtaining a good description of the suspect from the victim, clearly identifying any property stolen, speaking with witnesses and checking local CCTV expeditiously, may all be key to an early capture of the robber(s). Often gangs will target vulnerable and/or lone victims, so there may be more than one offender.

Upon the report of a robbery being committed the entire shift on duty (in some cases that's both of us) will flood the area like a crime-busting tsunami in search of any likely offender(s) matching the victim's description of them. Ideally the police want to catch a suspect near the offence location, matching the description passed, with the stolen property still on them for the greatest chance of a successful prosecution.

Robberies, like burglaries, can have a terrifying effect on the injured party. Although often not the case, it is hard for any victim not to take the crime personally, as such the experience may have an untold negative impact on their future life and outlook. If great trauma is caused to the victim this should be well documented in the statement they provide (usually taken by the front-line officer) as this will be taken into consideration when the offender is caught and subsequently punished – after all, wealth and material things can be easily replaced; confidence and happiness cannot.

Later on – even if the offender was arrested at the time – forensic DNA swabs might be taken from any surfaces which the offender could have touched, such as wallets, phones *and* the victim's jaw. The victim's clothes may also be seized by police (as if they haven't lost enough already that day) and forensically searched for traces of DNA, clothing fibres, or anything else that might lead to the suspect being identified. This is done even if a suspect is in custody, as in most cases the crime will be only witnessed by the victim themselves, and any corroborative evidence to support their account is important, especially if the victim does not know their attacker by name.

In reality though forensic investigation such as scientifically analysing DNA profiles from swabs and clothing samples at a suitably equipped laboratory is a time-consuming and costly exercise and – although the samples will still always be taken regardless, just in case – unless the crime is a particularly horrific one or the item lost is very high value, the chances are that samples will just sit in a police property store (in the case of the clothing) or a fridge at the station (for DNA swabs) gathering dust, never making it as far as the lab. If unsolved these samples will be kept for up to several years by which time the police have lost interest in the case they relate to and the victim has probably forgotten we still have them, before all is destroyed in an environmentally friendly way.

Hot Property

At this juncture I will interject to just quickly tell you about the police property store. Every station has one, and ours is situated deep down in the bowels of the building, in what resembles an old boiler room and looks like somewhere Freddie Kruger might frequent. Often fresh-faced probationers are sent down there to find a non-existent property reference number as someone else stands at the top of the stairs and turns the lights out – the screams can be heard all the way up on the third floor (oh the fun we have)!

The police love seizing stuff. We are like collectomaniacal magpies: we will seize anything. Partially because it just might prove useful to an investigating officer at a later date, but mostly because we'll only get criticised later on if we didn't take it. For example, somewhere hidden in our property store is a dented copy of the *Sex In The City* DVD box-set that you will hear about later.

The property store is like an Aladdin's Cave, full of all sorts of paraphernalia. From Nintendo Wiis to ornamental trees, samurai swords to bedroom drawers, baseball bats to cowboy hats, we have it all. As well as enough weapons to arm a rebel force, we also have more TV's than Dixons, more mobiles than The Carphone Warehouse, as well as enough drugs to make Tony Montana green with envy.

It always astounds me how many baseball bats there are in this country. I don't know anyone who plays the sport, yet most cars cruising around the Chavington Manor estate late at night have at least one in the boot. Maybe it's a sign of the decline in national traditions that not more cricket bats are the weapon of choice out in the urban jungle. Call me a sentimental old fool but if lunatic thugs must spend their evenings violently bludgeoning each other half to death, why not show a bit of national pride and use a good old-fashioned cricket bat? After all, the gentlemanly game of cricket has been played throughout this fair land since Tudor times in the early 16th century. Maybe in time, said thugs would come to love the hallowed sound of willow on skull...

I digress.

A brave civilian property officer is employed with the unenviable task of bringing some semblance of order to the chaos by logging entry and movements of the various sporting goods and other property. The force could probably solve the problem of its budget deficit if we sold half the junk we've accumulated, but that would be immoral and wrong – so much like fudging figures for the Home Office then.

11. I See Dead People

A 'Sudden Death' (sometimes referred to as an 'unexpected death') is any death where the person has died and at that exact time of passing it was unexpected. This could mean anything from a tragic accident like someone falling off a ladder, a pre-meditated suicide, or even an 80-year-old passing away peacefully whilst sleeping at home having been fit and well(ish) though the day before.

Some new recruits to the police service will probably not have even seen a dead body before. The prospect of beholding and sometimes smelling a dead body is often one of the biggest concerns for people coming into the job and a subject people ask about all the time. I cannot sugar coat it – as a police officer you'll see some truly harrowing and traumatic sights: you will see people with horrific injuries that will change their lives forever, as well as those whose life expired many weeks before they were found. No officer enjoys attending sudden death jobs, but with the support of your colleagues and other avenues available (such as the welfare department that every force has) the impact of the unpleasant jobs is eased. Even the most hardened veteran officer would still admit the untimely death of a child is the worst possible incident a police officer can be asked to deal with; but this is what makes the police officer such a rare and unique breed – why we join up: because we have the inner strength and resolve to tread where others fear to.

*FACT: Every incident police are likely to attend has a written Standard Operating Procedure (SOP). Officers can refer to SOP's for guidance as to how certain incidents are to be treated and subsequent police actions to be taken. What follows is a **very*** *abbreviated SOP for a Sudden Death occurrence intended purely as an example.*

- *Officers attend scene promptly. Scene is secured to prevent loss of evidence and ambulance service to be called immediately. If applicable, officers may attempt resuscitation as per first aid training.*
- *If resuscitation unsuccessful, paramedics or qualified medical officer will confirm death and time life pronounced extinct.*
- *All events and actions to be recorded by police officers in attendance.*
- *Whilst carefully preserving evidence, officers to search scene for signs of suspicious death. In the event of any evidence coming to light to suggest this, senior supervisors along with SOCO to be contacted immediately and all evidence left in situ. Suicides, overdoses, violent deaths, industrial accidents, as well as unexplained and infant deaths will all be routinely referred to CID for their consideration.*
- *If deemed non-suspicious, police will attempt to contact next of kin (NOK) for deceased. Ideally NOK will formerly identify deceased to officers.*
- *Once scene has been released by senior officers, undertakers may be called to remove body to a designated mortuary where the local coroner will take responsibility. Police officer in attendance will create a report for the coroner which must be available as soon a practicably possible.*
- *The body will remain the responsibility of the coroner until released to the NOK.*

The primary role of an attending police officer at a sudden death is to establish if there is any suspicion of foul play before acting as an agent on behalf of the local coroner. The police always attend incidents considering the worst case scenario, and work back from there; so every sudden death is a potential murder, just as even the most minor assault could deteriorate into a serious injury later on. A call handler along with control room supervisors will decide from the outset if a sudden death is likely to be suspicious: if the informant (who most likely will be the ambulance service as that's who most MOPs call first, before the ambulance in turn inform the police) reports a sharp metallic object is sticking out the back of the person who is no longer breathing, this would be deemed suspicious, and someone with at least stripes (a sergeant) will also be dispatched. Otherwise the humble PC will usually suffice. Some forces will demand a supervisor attends *every* sudden death, irrespective of the suspiciousness.

Assuming nothing too untoward jumps out from the initial information received, the (most likely reluctant) constable will head to the address where the deceased has been found. Firstly it is important to establish that the untimely departed is in fact definitely dead (it's quite embarrassing and awkward for all concerned if you get this wrong); usually a paramedic will perform an ECG (electrocardiogram – an electrical contraption with wires to be attached via electrodes to various places on a person's body) on the subject to confirm this, irrespective of obvious degree of rigor mortis and sometimes decomposition – I once saw a paramedic place the ECG electrode stickers on a body with maggots crawling out of the poor man's face! When the paramedic removed the sticky pad a small lump of the man's chest came with it!

Paramedics will complete a brief statement confirming their actions and when death was pronounced, which is handed to the PC for the coroner's report.

Once death has been confirmed and the time and

paramedic's details who confirmed 'life extinct' has been recorded, it's time to get gloved up; the body has to be searched in entirety – literally from head to toe – for any signs of injury that might be contributory to the person's cardiac arrest. A humble police constable is not expected to determine cause of death – that's for the coroner to decide – but you don't have to be Quincy to work out if certain injuries are a little dubious. Also the locality, or 'scene', in which the body is located should also be searched for any signs of a struggle, suicide notes, evidence of drug use, etc.

Next it's time to find out about the legacy the deceased has left behind. It's time to speak to the people who found the body and the next of kin if they are not the same person. Information about pre-existing medical conditions, medication taken, or recent decline in the deceased's health should be recorded and will all be included on the coroner's report. For many experienced officers the sight of a dead person, or even having to discreetly search the body, doesn't bother them in the slightest because, without deliberately sounding cold-hearted and insensitive, they are professional and didn't know them. But I am human (like most police officers) so I might find having to ask grieving family members personal and sometimes intrusive questions about their loved ones is not pleasant. For example, asking a hard-working, upstanding, middle-aged, grieving mother about her recently deceased delinquent son's class A drug habit is incredibly awkward – especially when the body is still in the next room with a syringe sticking out of their arm.

Finally, having established all the facts for the coroner's report, the undertakers can be summoned to remove the body to the mortuary. In most cases, the undertakers will be appointed by the council whose jurisdiction the death occurred in. The length of the officer's presence once undertakers are called depends on individual force's policies. Some allow officers to leave as soon as a 'non-suspicious' death is confirmed and coroner's report completed, whilst others require their officers to follow the undertaker's private ambulance all the way to the mortuary where the coroner takes custody of the body until they release it back to the family for funeral arrangements.

Rest in Peace

It's been cold for the last few days. Each morning this week has started with a heavy frost, the first of the year, and drivers have lost the ability to commute sensibly (as is the annual tradition) and now crash regularly every rush hour. Having just finished with the latest road traffic collision (RTC) I am asked to attend 13 Apollo Close: the neighbours have not seen Mr Worthers for weeks now, the post is building up under the letter box, his dog barks constantly and, until the recent frost, there where blue bottles at the windows is the information passed over the radio. Ominous alarm bells are already ringing in my head.

Within a fraction of a second of my acknowledgement to the radio controller, my colleague PC Smith chirps up on the radio and eagerly offers to bring down the 'big universal key' just in case Mr Worthers is in no position to come to the door.

Smithy is a big lad, a gym member, has a spiky boy-band haircut, regularly drinks protein shakes, has to wear long sleeve shirts to cover his tattoos, and has no interest whatsoever in paperwork. He is however full of wanton for destruction and always available to smash a front door to oblivion when the needs must. Smithy is also very handy in a scrap and has gotten me out of a few scrapes on many an occasion. By no means the brightest crayon in the box but still a very good mate of mine and a true firearms officer in waiting!

The big universal key, AKA 'The Enforcer', Smithy refers to is basically the metal battering ram you have no doubt seen used in dawn drug raids during fly-on-the-wall TV documentaries. Its use is usually succeeded by words along the lines of, "POLICE! GET DOWN ON THE FLOOR! NOBODY MOVE!" In this instance, I fear the occupant of the house, Mr Worthers, may already be on the floor and not have moved for some time! PC Smith is already pre-empting the need to force open the old chap's door and tells the control room he will meet me at the address.

The Enforcer is part of the Method of Entry (MOE) kit – specialist tools used to gain entry, usually by force, to an otherwise secure building. Officers are specially trained to use this. Another option from the MOE bag of tricks is a piece of equipment called 'The Rabbit' (calm down ladies); this is a hydraulic device used to prise open doors and their frames. Highly effective against uPVC doors in particular, it can sometimes pop open a door with no damage caused at all. For this reason it is seldom used by Smithy as he would argue, "What's the fun in that?"

I arrive at the quiet cul-de-sac and let Control know as I do. The address history checks I requested are relayed to me via the radio operator.

I'm told police haven't been called to the address for five years and then it was to assist the ambulance service who had a male with chest pains refusing to attend hospital. That incident was concluded when the male had a reluctant change of heart and off he went, but no names or phone numbers are mentioned. Every time police attend an address, a computerized log is held so that in the future officers can draw upon any useful information from that historic archive. This information is often very helpful and can give an idea of whom an officer is likely to encounter on arrival at an address – but unfortunately not in the case of 13 Apollo Close.

The house itself is a dingy looking end terrace. The curtains are all drawn and the small front garden is unkempt. Ever the optimist, I ring the doorbell, and ever the pessimist knock the door as I'm sure the bell won't work (they never do). No answer. There's a similar story at the rear with dirty looking net curtains obscuring my view and dog business dotted around the overgrown lawn like little land mines laid specifically for unsuspecting police officers.

Returning to the front I now give the door a 'policeman's knock' – like a regular knock but excessively hard and loud. Still no answer. There's also no sign of the animal that littered the back garden with booby traps either. Bending down I lift the letterbox flap and inhale; I'm trying to detect that oh-so-familiar, indescribable but unforgettable stench – dead person. Tragic to say but any police officer will tell you the smell of a decomposing body is unique, pungent and will linger on an officer's skin, clothes and hair for the rest of a shift until a much needed shower is had. The house smells musty and unpleasant but this can't conclusively be attributed to a rotting homeowner inside.

Whilst I wait for my door knocker (PC Smith) to arrive, I make the routine enquiries with neighbours. As I knock on the first few doors, Smithy arrives. He gets out of his panda car and starts flexing his muscles in anticipation of the violence to secure entry he hopes to soon use.

Meanwhile I'm talking to Doris who lives next door. She tells me she called us and goes on to say that

Mr Worthers keeps himself to himself and they hardly ever see him except when he's walking his dog – Snowflake. He never has visitors and she does not know of any family. Doris continues to say she thinks he likes a drink, raising a snooty eyebrow as she gossips whilst making the 'drinky-drinky' motion to illustrate her point. All the other neighbours must be dicing with death on the highways as no one else is at home.

I report back my findings to the control room and they advise me Mr Worthers has not been admitted to any of the local hospitals, nor is he currently in police custody somewhere (the same routine checks done for missing people you may recall). I look at Smithy and shrug my shoulders. A wry smile spreads across his face. Having exhausted all avenues preventing Smithy from doing what he does best, I have no option but to unleash him on the wooden threshold. He takes up position by the door, steadies himself with enforcer in both hands, slowly swings back, before launching the lump of metal forward with enough excessive force to destroy a small building, striking the door just below the lock.

With an almighty bang the whole house shakes and the door smashes open almost coming off its hinges.

We both stare down the hallway, wide eyed in fright: there, on the dirty lino, just a few feet from us, with its back arched, teeth bared, is the biggest, blackest, angriest, snarling dog I've ever seen. This must be Snowflake. Smithy and I look at each other for a second, before we both turn and run back to my panda with 'Cerberus' in hot pursuit. I think I might even have sworn, but couldn't hear myself over Smithy screaming like a terrified schoolgirl as he runs down the path, arms flapping like a demented duck, before clawing at the car door handles to get inside. The squealing noise made by my macho comrade was so high pitched I was surprised it was not only audible to Snowflake. His exhibition of terror combined with cowardice was nothing short of spectacular and will remain with me for the rest of my life, bringing much needed amusement on even the most bleakest of scene guards.

We both jump into the police car, me in the front and my excitable colleague in the back, slamming the doors shut behind us. I turn to see Snowdrop has stopped in the doorway of his master's house, now barking furiously in an uncontrollable rage at the two intruders.

After a few minutes Snowdrop desists and sits in the open doorway, but still watching us intently. Thinking now is my opportunity I gently open the panda door. As soon as my foot touches the frosty pavement below Snowdrop again arches his back, bears his teeth and begins to growl once more. I close my panda door.

"What are you going to do now then?" enquires Smithy, slouching back in his seat behind me and clearly washing his hands of the whole sorry affair.

"I'm open to suggestions," I reply.

"Have you got a bone?" is Smithy's offering.

I don't know if he was serious or not but the look of contempt and irritation I send his way is enough to stop any more helpfulness coming from PC Smith's direction. I start to reach for my radio to update control but quickly withdraw my hand when I realise: why on earth would I want to share my current predicament with the rest of the radio channel? They're still ribbing me about 'Mad Marygate'!

Sitting imprisoned in the police car I ponder for a few moments my next move. Offering up Smithy as a human sacrifice is not really a viable option, but suddenly it dawns that he might be on to something with his previous suggestion: I don't have a bone in my possession, but I do have a corned beef and pickle sandwich – a guilty pleasure of mine which I bought from home. Police officers don't really get a lunch hour – inconsiderate victims aren't prepared to wait for 45 minutes at knife point whilst I finish my pot noodle and idly flick through the Heat magazine someone has left in the canteen – so I carry my pack up around with me in the glove box.

I was looking forward to my sandwich but resign myself to the fact sacrificing my 'refs' (refreshments/food) might be a better alternative to spending the rest of my shift captive in the car until I swallow my pride and call for assistance on the radio (there's no way the hound is getting my Monster Munch and Curly Wurly though!) I'd much prefer to offer up Smithy's refs to the mutt, but I don't think Snowflake would go for a plastic shaker bottle with a pink sports nutrition powder in the bottom; besides, that's in the police car parked a good 10 metres away and I'm sure Snowflake would tear me limb from limb before I even got half way.

Unwrapping my sandwiches from the cling film, I slowly open the vehicle door. Snowflake immediately begins to growl disapprovingly and primes himself to feast on raw police officer. I close my panda door once more. Instead I wind down the electric window.

"Good boy, Snowflake. Do you want some lunch?" I gingerly say.

Snowflake is barking in my direction like a rabid maniac again. Clearly not the one for small talk, so instead I carefully toss out my meagre offering which lands just in front of him. Snowflake wolfs down the first triangle in half a second flat and the second quickly follows.

Now with a far more satisfied look on his face, a nourished Snowflake sinks to the floor appearing much more contented.

"He looks like he enjoyed that," points out the ever attentive Smithy.

"Yeah, shall we get out and see if his mood has improved?"

"You can, good luck," says my ever supportive crew mate.

After a couple of minutes, I slowly, for the third time, open the panda door to take my chances with the beast. Snowflake is still suspicious of me as I tentatively approach but refrains from tearing my flesh from bone. As I get within a few feet Snowflake again arches his back but isn't nearly as ferocious as before.

"Good boy, there's a good boy," I nervously mutter.

Mustering all my courage I gently reach out towards Snowflake. Whereas pre sandwich he would no doubt have severed my hand right now, Snowflake seems to have warmed to me and lets me pat him on the head without even biting off a digit. I sigh with relief and boldly take my new K9 companion by the collar and gently usher him towards the stair-gated kitchen and fill up his bone-dry water bowl at the sink. I leave Snowflake lapping frantically at the water as I back away and secure him behind the gate.

Outside I can see Smithy peering out from the sanctuary of the police car. I'm tempted to leave him in there as rear doors on police cars only open from the outside (we lose too many prisoners otherwise) but instead I decide to release him – but only so he can help me search the house as, after all, that is what we came for.

Having overcome the Snowflake obstacle, Smithy and I can take in the Worthers' residence – what a dump. As well as huge piles of dog excrement scattered all over the filthy carpet, there are empty alcohol bottles, food packets and cigarette butts everywhere. The house has an horrific aroma too.

"Someone should clear up a bit in here," PC Smith is on fine form today.

"OK Smithy, if we find him I'll mention that."

"Maybe it's the maid's day off?"

Smithy and I go about searching the house and call out to Mr Worthers. No sign downstairs. I apprehensively creep upstairs fearing the worst.

As I get to the landing I see him. Mr Worthers, or that's who I presume he is, is lying face down and naked in the doorway to the bedroom. I can see poor Mr Worthers' life has long been extinct. His back is grey whilst his lower side is green, purple and swollen where his bodily fluids have sunk down. Liquid is leaking from somewhere but I can't see where. The smell is overpowering so I try to breathe through my mouth, but then I can taste the decay instead so try to just hold my breath as long as possible. I call down to Smithy to tell him what I've found before putting on latex gloves. I have a quick look around the body for any signs consistent with a suspicious death but have no intention of searching the corpse – Mr Worthers clearly passed on some months ago and now unfortunately he presents a biohazard to anyone who comes into contact with him.

His face is black, I see his eyes have melted away from their sockets, and dry blood is running from his mouth. I go back downstairs, take a deep breath, update police control room and summon a paramedic to confirm death.

I warn Smithy it's not a pretty sight upstairs but that does not stop him taking a nosey look. He quickly comes back down slightly greener than before and now retching. It dawns on me now why Snowflake was so hostile towards us upon arrival having probably been witness to his master's death and his only sustenance since having come from spoiled leftovers scattered about the house.

Whilst we wait for the paramedic to arrive, Smithy and I have the unenviable task of finding Mr Worthers' next-of-kin details. The house is in disarray with paperwork scattered everywhere. I find a six-month-old bank statement showing Mr Worthers account is over £11k in credit, but nothing that identifies any family, only out-of-date telephone numbers scribbled down on scraps of paper in an old address book. The paramedic arrives and completes the formalities of confirming time of death. I attach the relevant details to our computerised incident log via the radio as well as Mr Worthers' full name and date of birth which I found on old paperwork.

As is often the case with finds of this grizzly nature, the sergeant also pops along to have a nose and cast an authoritative eye over proceedings. After just five minutes our supervisor has surveyed the house, admired Smithy's handy work on the front door, noted the filth and alcohol bottles that wash across the scene, retched at the sight of the putrefying body upstairs before concurring that nothing suspicious is evident. She then leaves as quick as she came.

Unable to find any information leading to surviving family or even friends, the next people to join us are the undertakers which control room staff call. Wearing full disposable suits, two pairs of gloves each and masks across their faces, the two burly undertakers wrestle the stiff body into a zip up body bag and gradually maneuver it down the stairs and into the back of their private ambulance for the journey to the hospital mortuary. A local animal shelter volunteer turns up to take the now whimpering Snowflake away to be cared for and nurtured back to health. I give him a pat on the head as he is led away. It makes me smile as I see Smithy take a big step back, clearly still wary of Snowflake, as he passes by in the hallway. I will take great pleasure in telling the rest of the team about Smithy's cowardice later on so that they can join me in teasing the big man accordingly – they might now finally move on from my recent Mad Mary fiasco.

Finally, having seized the address book for the coroner to scrutinise thoroughly just in case next-of-kin details are contained within, and having obtained all I need for my report, a council maintenance contractor is called to repair the damage Smithy inflicted on the doorway and secure the house. Smithy waits at the house for the 'boarder-upper' whilst I return to the police station to prepare the coroner's report.

Back at the station I complete a statement about my findings and actions relating to 13 Apollo Close, as I anticipate a coroner's inquest will be held to confirm the cause of death, before I send it all off with the report to the coroner's office. Mr Worthers' sister was later traced and informed of the death of her brother by a police officer from a neighbouring county and force. A verdict was recorded of a natural death, hastened by alcohol abuse and neglect.

The tragic tale of Mr Worthers' demise is a harrowing one; clearly evident by the way he lived, he was unable to look after himself but, also as apparent, was that no one – family, friends or social services – intervened to offer support. He died alone months ago without anyone caring enough about him to realise. There are thousands of people just like Mr Worthers living in squalor without assistance – some have put themselves in that position, but others society has just turned its back on. Police officers come into contact all the time with individuals and families crying out for help; which we can provide indirectly by referring the people in need to partner agencies who can offer the support they so desperately crave. We are in a position where they can offer assistance and make a difference to people's lives. But sadly we were too late for Mr Worthers.

12. Investigation and Interrogation

I have some more controversy for you now:

The paperwork police officers have to contend with isn't that bad.

Ok, let me quantify that bold, sweeping statement: sure, there is enough bureaucracy, form-filling and duplication in the police to send even the sanest officer, stark raving bonkers with frustration – but then there are huge amounts of this in any public sector job. It would be fantastic if governments could 'cut the red tape', freeing up front-line police officers to proactively seek out criminals, but it's not going to happen any time soon, so modern 21st century officers just have to put up, shut and get on with it – after all, it's the British way!

Nothing generates paperwork more than a thorough and comprehensive investigation. It might surprise you to hear that the objective of a good investigation is not actually to gather as much damning evidence against the accused as possible but, in fact, to obtain a balanced account of *all* the evidence relating to the offence in question – even if some of that evidence undermines the prosecution's case (the prosecution are the good guys by the way i.e. the police and the Crown Prosecution Service). If a prolific and repeat offender states in interview whilst in custody that he couldn't possibly have robbed that old lady in the park because at that time he was volunteering down at the local soup kitchen helping the less fortunate, then the dedicated police officer in charge of the case is duty bound to investigate this claim and, however unlikely it sounds, gather evidence proving the alibi one way or another.

The onus is on the prosecution to prove the accused is guilty – not for the accused and his defence team to prove their innocence. Whether correct or not, this is the whole basis of our legal system – innocent until proven guilty.

It is not the police constable's job to apportion blame, pass judgment and decide if a prosecution is to proceed – that is the role of a custody sergeant or the Crown Prosecution Service (CPS). The ultimate decision on whether a conviction is possible and the subsequent proportionate punishment is then down to the courts. Their decision is influenced by the contents of the charge file which is compiled by the 'Police Officer In Case' (the OIC) on the advice and guidance of the CPS.

The police use a series of forms called 'Manual of Guidance' forms (or MG forms for short) that make up these files. These series of forms are designed to make building a case file structured and 'simplified' – but the process can still be incredibly perplexing! It is a bit like those fantasy role playing books you might have read as a teenager:

If you want to enter the dungeon and try to slay the dragon, roll the dice and turn to page 187.

Remember those? Instead the police version would go:

If you want to apply to remand your prisoner in custody, get yourself another coffee from the machine, extend your duty time a further 3 hours, then complete the MG4, MG5, MG6, MG7 and MG8 forms.

File-building does take time and experience to become competent at – I might even know what I'm doing myself with a file one day – but fortunately there are always experienced colleagues and supervisors who are available to guide a flummoxed officer back on the righteous path .

Justice Will Prevail (?)

In most cases a specialist investigation team will deal with prisoners in custody, as well as furthering investigation through to hopeful charge, and then on to a court trial if required. The specialist teams might be the prisoner handling units, or in more serious cases the Criminal Investigation Department (CID). Every police force will have their own procedures and practices, but all operate roughly the same way. Below is a simplified example of the justice system from the point a victim makes an allegation and/or a crime is committed, through to court and a hopeful conviction.

1. Complaint/Victim

To start an investigation you must have a victim (which might be an organization or the state if not an actual person) and preferably one prepared to provide a statement making a complaint and then to back it up by appearing in court if required. In some cases, particularly domestic violence ones, the victim will not be cooperative to police, nor provide a statement and will not support a prosecution of the offender. People often say they want to 'press charges' against someone who has wronged them and, although improper terminology for the UK, this is basically saying I will support the prosecution. After I point out to them they are not in America and should stop watching so much TV, I then take a statement of complaint from them which starts the creaky, worn out cogs of justice in motion.

2. Investigation

One word against another is sometimes enough to arrest someone, but it is much better if you actually have some evidence to support the complaint. As well as the victim's statement, evidence might also come in the form of CCTV footage, seized property, forensic findings, or witness testimonies. This can be a long-winded process but is often the foundations of the prosecution case and shortcuts might undermine all that follows so officers must be diligent.

3. Arrest and Interview

Once you have got enough evidence it is time for someone to get locked up. It probably shouldn't be, but for most officers arresting someone is a bit like scoring a goal – you get a buzz from it and it is one of the reasons they come to work. I often hear excitable and competitive officers in the locker room discussing how many arrests they have already for the month.

Once arrested, a suspect will be taken to their nearest police station with a custody suite and interviewed about the allegation. In interview the suspect has three options: tell the truth, make up a lie, or say nothing at all and go "no comment". The latter is becoming increasingly more common as wannabe gangsters see it on TV, as well as a habit of defence solicitors advising their clients to keep shtum for fear of saying something stupid in interview and incriminating themselves further.

In an ideal world we would now jump to stage 5, but often there is some tidying up to do in stage 4.

4. Further Investigation

Depending on what was said in interview and other

lines of investigation that have come to light, there might be the need to make further enquiries. This could be checking alibis or speaking with further witnesses. The suspect will most likely be released on bail, with a condition agreeing to return to the police station at a prearranged time and date in the future whilst the enquiries are made. Other bail conditions might be not to contact the victim, witnesses or go to certain places, or even to abide by home curfews for certain hours of the day to prevent further offences. In order to protect victims, witnesses, evidence or prevent further offences, the accused may instead be 'remanded in custody' (held in prison) until time comes to answer bail.

5. Charging Decision and Disposal

Finally, once a balanced investigation has taken place and all the required evidence is gathered, a decision about what to do next can be made. If a suspect has admitted an offence and has no previous convictions for similar offences they may be eligible for a penalty notice for disorder (or PND – basically a fine) or a caution and be released; not to be confused with the caution spoken when arresting someone; a caution in this context is an alternative to a full prosecution at court which, however, remains on an individual's police record indefinitely. How long a police caution lasts depends on the type of offence that has been committed and are usually 'stepped down' after about five to ten years depending on how serious the offence was. Once a caution has been stepped down, then it will only be viewed by the police and not by members of the public or any companies that do history checks such as Criminal Records Bureau (CRB) checks.

If they have been a naughty boy or girl in the past, then someone with authority to do so – usually a custody sergeant or the CPS – may decide they should be charged and sent to court.

The above resolutions are called 'positive disposals' and result in something called 'detections'. These are important as they aid a police force in climbing up the Home Office league table (and senior officer's to climb up the promotion ladder). Big bosses get very excited about detections – a solved crime is a tick in the box as far as the police are concerned, irrespective of what might happen at court where the accused may still be found not guilty! Among other things, detections are an easy way for the Home Office to make comparisons between forces and pass judgment on a force's performance, so great emphasis is placed on eking out every detection possible.

On the flip side, it might be decided that the poor accused is innocent of all crimes (or at least the police can't produce evidence to sufficiently prove they did it) and should be released back into society – normally with a leaflet in hand explaining how they go about making a complaint to the Independent Police Complaints Commission (IPCC) about their treatment whilst in custody and what they will now protest was an unlawful arrest. Arresting the right person is only half the battle; proving they did it is the real challenge.

6. Paperwork and the Court Process

Throughout the above stages several innocent trees will lose their lives unnecessarily as the investigating officer accrues copious amounts of paperwork. Once a conclusion to the case is achieved – positive or otherwise – the paperwork must be put together in a file and sent to the relevant people for either filing off into the ether never to be seen again, or sent to court along with the accused. If it's court for the scoundrel, a magistrate or judge and jury will either 1. find the accused innocent and release them without charge, 2. find them guilty but hand out a meagre punishment incentivizing the reprobate to commit further criminal activities as they got off so lightly this time or, 3. on very rare occasions, hand down a punishment proportionate to the crime committed so that justice is done and the victim recompensed.

Interviewing

Let me elaborate a little on stage 3 now. Every prisoner must be granted an opportunity to give their version of events – whether they seize that opportunity is up to them. In custody a taped interview will take place.

The prospect of sitting in a tiny sound-proofed room with an uncooperative villain and his knowledgeable solicitor by his side staring disdainfully at you is a daunting one. Throw into the mix and interview room the possibility of an interpreter and an appropriate adult and claustrophobic is not the word!

Student officers will be given many opportunities to interview prisoners as this is a key fundamental of being a police officer. Those young in service often give themselves a hard time if they do not manage to drive their suspects into submission Gene Hunt style and get a full and frank confession during interview. I did myself until an experienced CID officer enlightened me by pointing out obtaining a confession on tape is not necessarily the purpose of an interview; it is in fact to *'close doors'* on the suspect by asking relevant and considered questions giving them the opportunity to answer there and then, removing the chance to fabricate excuses at a later time. By simply asking a suspect in interview to thoroughly account for their actions regarding the circumstances of the crime they stand accused, the interviewer has done their job as any lies told by the suspect will hopefully be uncovered by thorough investigation prior or post interview. If a suspect then chooses to change his account from that given in interview, hopefully those passing judgment will see through the deceit accordingly.

TOP TIP: Thorough planning before an interview is vital as there will be more structure and flow as a result; also you are less likely to leave the interview thinking, "Why did I not ask that!?" Rather than specific questions, most experienced interviewers will have broader 'topics' listed on their notes to put to the defendant. By using this method the interviewer can be more flexible and thorough during questioning and is less likely to be thrown if the defendant comes out with an unexpected twist in his/her account. Asking 'open' questions – those which do not invite a simple yes or no answer from the defendant – is key.

Prompt and Effective Investigation

Let us return to the tale of Geoffrey Steeles. If you recall his sticky fingers had once again wound him up incarcerated at the police station, standing accused of shoplifting for the millionth time. I am now ready to interview Geoff so walk back down to custody to speak with the sergeant. I can see Geoff's not in his cell from the CCTV screen in the custody office.

"Where's Geoff, Sarge?"

"In the yard, having a fag," is the reply. Outrageous!

"I'm ready to interview him now."

"OK, his duty solicitor is already here, I'll tell them."

Geoff has surprisingly opted for legal representation on this occasion so has been granted the services of a duty defence solicitor, in this case Mr Detani from Capones Legal Defence law firm (a duty solicitor is one provided free of charge by the taxpayer to any prisoner whilst in custody). I've crossed blades with Mr Detani a few times before – most memorably when I was a fresh-faced probationary constable and he made a complete fool of me in interview. For this reason I don't like Mr Detani, but I'm far too proud (stubborn) to admit that he made me look such a wally on that day because he was by far better at his job than I was at mine.

Whilst Geoff breaches the smoking ban in the exercise yard with the full consent of the custody sergeant, I have to give 'disclosure' to his solicitor:

At the discretion of the interviewing officer (me), disclosure is the information and evidence which is shared with the defence solicitor. Other than a copy of the custody detention log (a computerized record of the prisoner's grounds for detention and their treatment thus far in custody) there is no obligation to tell the defence solicitor anything. However, if an officer plays their cards too close to their chest and no information is shared, the defence solicitor will most likely advise their client to give a 'no comment' interview (refusal to answer any questions) or to give a 'prepared statement' (a written account or reply to any accusations against them) and nothing more. Neither of these are necessarily detrimental to a successful prosecution, in fact a court may draw adverse inference (may see it as a sign of guilt) from the defendant's failure to provide an account and therefore evidence, however it is generally best if some verbal replies can be elicited from the suspect. If on the other hand too much evidence is disclosed to the defence, there is more opportunity for the defendant to concoct a plausible but untrue explanation.

I decide to disclose the following:

Mr Steeles was found in possession of concealed stolen property from a local supermarket and that the incident was captured on CCTV; I also show Mr Detani some stills from the CCTV footage showing the suspect which I printed out in advance.

As I believe Steeles is 'bang to rights' on this one, I am happy to share my evidence as I am optimistic there is a remote chance Geoff will 'cough' (admit) to the whole offence and save everyone any further unnecessary time and expense. How naïve I am sometimes ...

Next Geoff and Mr Detani will go into 'Consultation' together. This involves them being shut in a room on their own where they can reacquaint themselves, discuss today's events, and decide how best to try and get away with it.

Whilst Geoff and Detani are scheming, it's time for me to plan Geoff's downfall in the upcoming interview. My first task is to find an available interview room with a TV and DVD player capable of showing the CCTV footage. This is by no means an easy task in the police station custody suite but, on only the third attempt, I find a room with functioning equipment – maybe it is to be my lucky day after all.

Next I get my new and still sealed cassette tapes ready for the tape recorder machine. Many police stations still use old fashioned tape recorders for two reasons:

1. Tapes are practically impossible to tamper with or edit so a pedantic defence solicitor cannot argue at court that the recording is doctored.
2. Police forces have no money to upgrade to digital systems anyway. Only the most affluent forces have digital recording technology.

There are three identical tapes used: the first will be a working copy used by the prosecution, the second a copy for the defence should they request it, and the final tape will be sealed with a label and only opened at the request of the court during a trial if it is required.

Now having my tapes and labels in order, it's time to plan my interview.

After half-an-hour, and just as I'd boiled the kettle in custody to have my well-deserved tea break, Geoff and his solicitor emerge from the consultation room and are ready for interview. The brew will again have to wait.

We are in interview room three. If you haven't seen an interview room on some police drama, they are basically tiny rooms with a table, a few chairs, a tape machine, and walls covered in special soundproofing material/carpet. There are also panic buttons on the walls for the benefit of the interviewer should the interviewee make a bolt across the table and try to disembowel the officer with his own biro. Geoff's far too old and brittle for any of those shenanigans so I should be fine.

So I am sitting in my chair, with my interview book in front of me, my topics of discussion listed, and biro in hand to note down the lies I anticipate might shortly be launched at me over the table. Sitting the other side is an emotionless, thieving old man and his stone-faced legal adviser. Having unwrapped the tapes from their seals and placed them in the recorder I am ready to begin.

"Mr Steeles, are you ready to be interviewed?"

"Yes, lad."

There is a short buzzing noise as the tape winds on before I start the long spiel required at the beginning of any interview. I start by stating my name, rank and collar number, the time and date, the interview room number we find ourselves in, before asking the defendant to identify himself in full.

"Mr Geoffrey Horatio Horace Tarquin Steeles, date of birth 20th February 1948, and I live at 23b High Road."

Next it is the turn of the legal representative to introduce himself.

"I am Mr Vinod Detani of Capones Legal Defence and I am here to represent Mr Steeles and see that he is treated fairly," is the somewhat pompous introduction.

Having checked Mr Steeles and his legal tipster have had sufficient time to confer, I remind Geoff (as if he needs it) of the offence he has been arrested for and emphasize he is still under caution before confirming he understands this. With the formalities over we can get down to the nitty-gritty of the interview.

"OK Geoff...," Detani glares at me disapprovingly, "... OK Mr Steeles, in your own words, explain to me what happened today leading up to your arrest?"

Rubbing his scruffy, grey face foliage pensively, Geoff starts to recollect.

"Well, Squire, I got up this morning, it was such a lovely day, I put on my best clothes, combed my hair, and ate some corn flakes. Semi-skimmed milk mind, Doctor says I have to watch my cholesterol. After that I decided I'd go to the park and feed the ducks as I often do. I feed them bread – mind you, some say you shouldn't do that; they say if the little ducklings eat bread it can swell up inside their stomachs and kill them. I think that's rubbish as I've always fed them bread and they hardly ever die. Anyway, I'm about to feed the ducks..."

"Mr Steeles! If I can interject, can you perhaps start from the bit where you go to the supermarket," I assertively interrupt.

"I was just getting to that, sonny, hold your horses. As I was saying, I was gonna feed the ducks but I had no bread. So what I did was go to the supermarket and get some. Anyway, I'm in that shop no more than a few minutes when two gorilla security guards grab hold of me and cart me off to an office saying I've stolen something! Well I couldn't believe it in all my days. Me, steal something? Next thing I know, you've turned up, whisked me off to the police station, and thrown me into a cell," is the convoluted, dubious and unconvincing explanation Geoff offers up.

"So you're saying you got up today with the intention of feeding ducks and went into the supermarket to get bread?" I summarise.

"Yes, Boss. I swear it to be true."

"Ducks?"

"Yes, Boss."

"Really?"

"To be sure."

"You say you regularly feed the ducks?"

Geoff nods. "Yes, guvnor."

"Which park were you going to feed these ducks at?" I have to confess, I'm not sure why I'm asking about ducks right now.

"Dickens Park, the one with the pond."

"That's about 3 miles from the supermarket I arrested you in..." I try to make a point.

"I need the exercise. Doctor says I should walk more. It's my arthritis in my back – he says I need more exercise."

Attempting to pull the interview back on track:

"When you were arrested you had no money and no bank card on you; how did you intend to pay for the bread you claim you entered the store to buy?"

"Did I not? Well blow me, I'd forget my head if it wasn't screwed on! Doctor says I should get more Vitamin B and Omega 3," Geoff chuckles, not fooling anyone.

"When you were arrested, I searched you and found various grocery items totalling £60.02 concealed in your clothing. About the only thing you didn't have on you was any bread. What do you have to say about that?" I go on the offensive.

"Well like I said, my memory's not so good. Fish is good for Vitamin B and Omega 3 you know," Geoff rambles. "I must have picked those other items up and forgot to pay for them. It was an honest mistake," protests Geoff holding his hands out in innocence.

Mr Detani sits next to Geoff nodding his head in agreement with his client.

"Who do those grocery items belong to?" I ask.

"Dunno, what groceries?"

"The groceries you stole. Could they belong to the supermarket, perhaps?"

"Dunno, what supermarket?"

"The supermarket you stole from. Have you been to that store before?" I continue.

"Not sure," says Geoff putting on a ponderous look, holding his hairy chin again and looking up in thought. "I can't recall."

Geoff's theatrical performance is wasted as there are no cameras in the interview room, but he seems to be enjoying his amateur dramatics so I don't mind.

"You have Mr Steeles, you've been arrested there many times before," I retort.

"If you say so, lad," Geoff replies, before Mr Detani interrupts.

"My client is here only to answer questions in relation to the offence he has been arrested on suspicion of today."

Mr Detani is right – I can't make reference to Geoff being arrested before at this stage of the interview and that last question will inevitably be omitted from the interview transcript by the tape summariser at a later date. Because Geoff has been arrested and dealt with for those countless previous offences, and as such been 'suitably punished and rehabilitated', any reference to the previous incidents heard by the court could cause potential prejudice and therefore be unfair. Previous convictions are usually only heard by the court for sentencing purposes.

"Do you know where the tills are in the supermarket? They're clearly marked."

"Well of course, I'm not an idiot, Sonny." Geoff's tone has changed – he seems a little sterner now as he sighs – clearly his patience is waning and interest fading.

Meanwhile Detani sits next to him tutting away, sighing in an exaggerated manner sounding like he is having an asthma attack, and shaking his head dismissively at my every question in an attempt to throw my concentration.

"I'm going to show you some CCTV from the store now, for the benefit of the tape (this is a fantastic interview room cliché!) can you describe to me what you're wearing now?"

As Steeles is wearing the same now as on the CCTV footage, it is important this is recorded in case the offender's identification was in question. Geoff sighs again before replying petulantly, but in fairness also rather comically:

"I'm wearing a pink leotard, tutu, and matching leggings."

I can't help smirking a little. That would actually be an even more eccentric get-up that what he is really wearing.

Suddenly though, just when I thought I had my adversary on the back foot and I can go in for the kill, Geoff launches a counter strike. At first it is just a slightly unpleasant aroma I can detect, but then the full force of Geoff's chemical-biological attack hits me! His face didn't even flinch. Detani subtly shuffles away from his client but other than a stifled cough he remains stone-faced and professional. With my eyes watering, my composure is momentarily rocked as I contemplate what Geoff could have eaten to produce such a fowl stench!

This is a highly unorthodox defensive interview technique and one I've never experience before – it is however proving highly effective as I struggle to breathe, my nostrils sting and my concentration waivers!

Refocusing I get back to the task at hand and Geoff's appearance.

"Erm ... that's simply not true, Mr Steeles," clearing my throat, "you are in fact wearing a brown hat, tweed jacket, yellow t-shirt and pale green trousers. Aren't you?"

"No I'm not."

"Yes you are."

"Am not."

My hope before the interview that Geoff might give me a full admission was not as deluded and far-fetched as it might have seemed; defendants are incentivized by the courts to admit offences at the earliest opportunity in return for lesser sentences. Unfortunately though Geoff is now instead completely uncooperative and making a mockery of everything, but I press on regardless.

"I'm going to show you exhibit BG1, CCTV footage from the supermarket leading up to your arrest."

"Any popcorn?" Geoff responds, rolling his eyes, "I like a good comedy."

We sit through five minutes of grainy CCTV footage – but it doesn't have to be in 1080p HD quality to see Geoff clearly stuffing various items of produce in his jacket like he is on *Supermarket Sweep*, bypassing the payment points, before being apprehended at the exit.

"Who's that in the footage with the beard, Mr Steeles?" I press home ruthlessly.

"No idea. Looks a little like Noel Edmunds to me."

"No, it's not the host of *Deal or No Deal* – It's you, Mr Steeles, isn't it?"

"No, no, you're right," Geoff squints at the screen

pretending to take a closer look, "it's not Noel Edmunds after all: it's definitely Jeremy Beadle."

I could point out it couldn't possibly be the late TV practical joker, but instead I go for the final challenge to shortly bring proceedings to an end.

"I put it to you that you went into the supermarket with the intention to steal various items which you hid in your clothes, before leaving making no attempt to pay. You knew the items belonged to the supermarket and had to be paid for in full but took them anyway to keep for yourself. What do you have to say about that?"

"Nothing. Can I go back to my cell now? Tea with five sugars please, Sonny."

After an exaggerated and intense pause for dramatic effect I ask Geoff if there is anything he wishes to add. He shrugs his shoulders dejectedly, so without further ado, I announce the time on my watch and terminate the interview.

I hand Geoffrey over to a detention officer for him to be 'processed' whilst I bid adieu to my nemesis – the slimy Detani – until the next time we tussle.

The detention officer will process Geoff by taking his photograph, fingerprints and drug test him for Class A drugs.

The purpose of the photograph is an obvious one. Fingerprints are taken every time a prisoner comes into custody because, despite popular opinion to the contrary, fingerprints can change over time albeit generally only through injury and scarring.

Theft-related crimes, called acquisitive crime, have been linked to drug use which costs the economy millions. As a result and in an attempt to place drug users and criminals into rehabilitation projects The Home Office now allows police forces to drug test prisoners in custody (aged 18-and-over only) arrested for acquisitive crimes – like shoplifting. A positive drugs test will result in compulsory attendance at a drug intervention centre. Failure to allow a test or adhere to drug rehabilitation will eventuate in a police charge.

FACT: A report by the Audit Commission found that half of all crime in England and Wales is in some way drug-related. It is estimated that drug users in the UK raise up to half a billion pounds a year through crime to fund their addictions. It has also been suggested that between one third to over a half of all acquisitive crime is related to illegal drug use and that there have been recorded examples of users needing £15,000 to £30,000 a year to fund drug habits.

POWER: Section 23 of the Misuse of Drugs Act 1971 provides powers to search and obtain evidence. If a constable has reasonable grounds to suspect that any person is in possession of a controlled drug, they may search that person. Furthermore, if a justice of the peace (that's a magistrate to you and me) can be satisfied by an officer swearing on oath that there is sufficient evidence to enter (by force is necessary) and search a premises for drugs they will grant an appropriate search warrant for the police to execute.

We will also take footwear impressions of Geoff's sandals. Shoes and trainers, a little like fingerprints, are unique too. Although tread patterns on footwear might seem the same as any other identical make, overtime small nicks and abrasions in the soles will make their footprint unique and recognisable. SOCO officers are able to take impressions at crime scenes of foot prints and if they match with a pair of footwear that has been seen on a prisoner in custody, or at some time in the future does appear on a prisoner, then that prisoner will have some explaining to do.

Finally a sample of DNA is taken from every prisoner via a painless mouth swab. Again this is done for speculative searches at past and future crime scenes. DNA does not change over a lifetime so a sample is only ever taken once.

The practice of taking photographs, fingerprints and DNA from every prisoner who comes into custody in England and Wales is a controversial one. This personal data is held indefinitely, irrespective of whether a suspect is found to be involved with the crime they stand accused or not. Human rights movements have argued that it is unfair for personal data to be kept of those when no further police action is taken against them; however until a government decrees otherwise the practice will continue.

Whilst Geoff's being given the once over by the detention officer, I speak with the custody sergeant in anticipation of a charging decision. I explain to the sarge that Geoff has denied everything in interview and did in fact suggest I redirect my investigation towards a couple of Saturday night primetime TV presenters from the 1990's, however I also go on to explain there is conclusive CCTV footage of the incident clearly showing Geoff's most recent bout of payment amnesia at a local supermarket. I refrain from bringing up the prisoner's outrageous outburst of flatulence during the interview as further evidence to support a charge of this most horrible of human beings.

If the sergeant was in any doubt about Geoff's guilt, he would condemn me to a good hour or so of form-filling followed by at least a two-hour wait for a phone call back from the Crown Prosecution Service for advice and a charging decision. Fortunately the sheer weight of evidence against Geoff, not to mention his incomparable track record for similar offences, means the custody sergeant has no hesitation in having me charge Geoff and send him to the local magistrate's court where no doubt another slap on the wrist will follow.

Charging a prisoner involves reading out verbatim the crime the prisoner stands accused of along with which law or 'Act' that particular crime contravenes – in Geoff's case the Theft Act of 1978. Immediately after informing the prisoner of their charge, they are verbally cautioned one more time and given a final opportunity to add anything else they would like to say in the form of a reply.

Geoff's charged for the umpteenth time and bailed to court with conditions not to enter any retail premises in town. Somehow I feel that despite Geoff's promise – which is basically what agreeing to a bail condition in custody is – my colleagues and I will be seeing the deviant pensioner again very soon.

13. Points Mean Prizes

A good thing about being a front-line divisional officer is that you can get involved in various and diverse areas of policing without necessarily restricting yourself to a specific role and/or department. Traffic policing and the offences that go with it is one such area that many officers find themselves gravitating to when on routine patrol – in between looking for missing teenagers, counselling couples over their domestic problems, and transferring thieving vermin from the streets and re-homing them in police stations (if only for a few hours at a time).

In most criminal law, offenders must have knowingly acted in a dishonest or deviant way for an offence to have taken place. For example, it is not a crime for someone to walk out of a store having not paid for an item if they are genuinely unaware of what they have done. The instant that person realizes what they have done and decides to keep the item instead of returning it, a theft has been committed and the forces of justice are coming for them (possibly)! Police and courts refer to this state of awareness as 'men srea' – Latin for 'guilty mind'.

Traffic offences on the other hand are far simpler to determine fault: it does not matter if the speeding motorist knew he/she had just entered a 30mph limit or not, or that he/she had a brake light out, or even that the phone call being made whilst driving was an essential one to the vets to find out how Bonzo the dog is after his big operation – traffic offences are 'absolute' and ignorance is not an excuse or defence against a ticket and prosecution.

The police are often criticized for not being tough enough on those who flagrantly break the motoring laws of the land, yet when it is the critics themselves who are on the receiving end of a £60 fine and 3 points for talking on their mobile phones, instead we should be finding better things to be doing with our time like locking up rapists, murderers and burglars. Believe me, police officers would much rather be out arresting child sex offenders than handing out tickets to those not wearing their seatbelts, but traffic law must be enforced as well.

POWER: A uniformed constable may stop any vehicle at any time under Section 163 of the Road Traffic Act 1988. Section 168 of the same act requires the driver of a vehicle to give their details to the police so that their identity can be confirmed along with their legal entitlement to be at the wheel of a motor vehicle.

As mentioned above, some traffic law is very straightforward; however other traffic law is slightly more complicated to follow than the storyline of *Lost*. Without dedicating many hours to reading legislation, even the most anal front-line officer will not know it all. Despite this fact, traffic law is the main topic friends, family and complete strangers alike will ask police officers about. The 'Great British Public' seems to assume officers know *everything* about *all* the laws! Often distant and slightly inebriated relations come up to me at weddings when they find out my profession and ask about trivial laws relating to towing weights of caravans, or HGV tachos, or tyre pressures, and expect me to immediately impart the answers from my encyclopaedic police mind. (What have lorries got to do with Mexican food anyway? Boom boom! Queue the short drum roll and cymbal crash!) When I cannot answer they seem so incredibly disappointed with me, like I have let them down. Then, when I in turn ask them what *they* do for a living and they tell me they are a hospital porter, and I ask them to explain to me how neurological surgery works in respect of the extra-cranial cerebrovascular system, often the ironic comparison I am making is lost on them. They usually make polite excuses and wander off again thinking I am very strange, regretting they spoke.

Drive It Like You Stole It

In the police you will get to drive all manner of vehicles on blue lights, at otherwise dangerous speeds, along public roads. Even after years of service, officers still get an adrenaline buzz from a good blue light run. As a crusader for justice you will get to drive someone else's car, that you do not have to fuel or maintain, at high speeds through busy streets, with little regard for the inconvenience caused to other motorists who have to move out of the way. Unfortunately the same can apply for the teenager behind the wheel of the car being chased in front.

During police driver training, officers learn that vehicle driving is an art form and safety and control is paramount. The aim of a good police driver is not necessarily to drive the fastest, but to drive within the limits of ability of the driver and vehicle and arrive at the destination in one piece.

During blue light runs the greatest obstacles presented to the police driver are the other cars on the road. Some members of the public seemingly go out of their way to impede police vehicles either through sheer panic or complete ignorance. As a police driver, I regularly encounter the following driver types every time I fire up the 'loud makers' (siren) on the Panda (small police cars driven by most divisional officers, so named due to traditionally being painted in black and white many years ago).

160

Ditch Divers AKA Curb Crunchers

A very common find on the highways and byways of Great Britain, these members of the public, to their credit, are in fact trying to be helpful when they see an illuminated police car quickly approaching in their rear-view mirror. Instead of applying indicators and calmly slowing down and moving out of the way, they make the decision to violently swerve their automobiles towards the curb causing untold damage to their alloy wheels and steering racks, not to mention terrifying the pensioner on the pavement trying to negotiate their way to Morrisons.

'Ditch divers' can evolve into 'oblivions' (see below) once the first Panda has overtaken them, but the second Panda following in convoy is still frustratingly stuck behind.

Emergency-Stoppers

Again – although trying to be accommodating – these motorists, when seeing a police car approaching to the rear, feel it is best to slam down hard on their middle peddle causing their car to grind to an immediate and tyre-smoking halt in the middle of the carriageway. Most standard police Panda vehicles are nothing more than family hatchbacks with reflective stickers on the side and empty McDonalds packaging in the footwells and door pockets. They are not upgraded at all as some might think. Their humble brakes cannot stop them on the proverbial sixpence, so instead emergency action must be taken to avoid the now fast-approaching Volvo Estate that has emergency-stopped right in front of them.

The Oblivions – "What Police Car?"

These are the motorists who are completely oblivious to the police car behind despite the blue LED lights strobing, headlights flashing and sirens blaring. They carry on regardless, driving along in their own little world with no knowledge of the police officer behind struggling to overtake to get to the violent domestic incident the other side of town. 'Oblivions' have even been known to overtake the car in front of them which *has* seen the approaching police vehicle two cars back and sensibly pulled over to the side of the road.

Please note, taxis and van drivers do not fall into this category: they are exempt from all traffic law and – a little known fact – are actually legally obliged to ignore any emergency vehicle displaying lighting and sounding sirens – or so I can only assume judging by their driving manner. (This must be another one of those complicated and mysterious traffic laws I spoke of earlier as I am still unaware of the exact legislation which this corresponds to.)

Mobile Chicanes

This is the most complex breed of driver to be found on Britain's roads. The experienced 'mobile chicane' driver will have the foresight to locate his or her car on a bend in the exact position that will cause a determined police driver the greatest possible inconvenience and danger.

An advanced form of this phenomena involves two similar-thinking drivers travelling in opposite directions. Although difficult to choreograph, when done successfully both drivers will stop their cars almost adjacent, with a gap barely a car's width between them, forcing the experienced police driver to attempt a form of car limbo through the hole created. If successful, the victorious officer may carry on his righteous journey; however, if unsuccessful, the officer has an awkward meeting with his/her supervisor to look forward to and a vehicle insurance form to complete.

Driving School

As a police driver, would-be Lewis Hamiltons hone their driving skills on comprehensive training courses usually conducted by expert serving police officers or adept civilians with past police experience. Their students are taught to drive to a tried and tested, strict system with emphasis on speed, accuracy and above all else safety. The courses – which are held on public roads – are intense and require great mental concentration as well as physical endurance. If the same courses were available to members of the public (which of course they are not!) they would cost thousands of pounds. Many officers will say the driving courses are the best and most enjoyable ever undertaken. Undoubtedly the comprehensive training, combined with the sight of road traffic crash victims, will make all police officers much improved and safer on the roads – even when in their own cars.

Generally speaking there are three grades of police driver:

> ***Non-Response*** – Most forces still put officers through a shortened examination of their driving ability which once completed allows the officer to drive marked ('stickered up') police vehicles but in a non-response capacity. This ultimately means they are restricted to driving by the

normal traffic laws of the land and are forbidden to use the emergency lighting. PCSOs whose forces allow them to drive marked vehicles also fall into this category.

People tend to notice police cars when they drive by – that's the idea of all the funky reflective liveries. For this reason forces place great emphasis on driver standards as mistakes or bad habits displayed by officers portray the force in a negative light. The British public holds their police service to high account and loves nothing more than to complain when they do not believe they are getting value for money from their hard-earned tax payments.

Standard Response – Most divisional officers will fall in to this category. These are the ones that can put on the blue lights and the 'nee-naas' to respond to emergency incidents, as well as pulling over cars when required. Generally speaking these officers can also take part in the initial stage of a police pursuit until a more qualified and better equipped unit (a traffic officer for example) can take over.

Pursuits are a potentially dangerous occurrence, not just to the police officers involved and the occupants of the 'subject vehicle' (the car being followed), but to other unsuspecting motorists, cyclists and pedestrians as well. A decision as to whether a vehicle 'failing to stop' for police should be pursued or not usually comes from a senior officer in the force's control room based on the information passed by the units on the ground who are following the vehicle. Factors such as weather conditions, traffic weight, time of day, the type of subject vehicle and the subject's driving style will all be taken into consideration as well. A decision will be made as to whether the high risk associated with a police pursuit is worth the effort to pursue and potentially apprehend the suspect, as sometimes it is not.

Advanced Response – Usually the reserve of specialist units like traffic, dog handlers or firearms officers. Having completed and passed a long training course where candidates must display exceptional driving ability and decision-making. 'Advanced' officers are equipped with superior vehicles so that they can get to where they need to go quickly.

Ably assisted by the police helicopter, these drivers are the crème-de-la-crème of roads policing and are called upon whenever a pursuit is, or is likely, to take place. The 'Interceptor' cars you have seen on TV are always piloted by advance-level officers.

Crash, Bang, Wallop

Attending road traffic collisions (RTC's) are a regular occurrence for front-line divisional officers. Traffic officers are only interested in RTC's that result in fatal or serious injury, have occurred on the motorway (where generally speaking regular officers in mere Pandas are forbidden to tread), or if a drunk person is involved who will need arresting. Anything else is fair game for a humble divisional police constable.

The primary consideration when arriving at an RTC is to assess if there are any casualties. If there are, then get a paramedic there ASAP as we already know how inadequate the basic police first aid training is! If there are no casualties then officers speak to drivers, passengers and witnesses to find out exactly what has happened. Drivers often stand next to their battered Ford Fiestas and say things like, "That's a dangerous bend really. I'm surprised there aren't more accidents," to excuse and exonerate themselves of blame.

Sometimes I agree: it might be a bad bit of road ... so slow down then! I refrain from pointing out thousands of other motorists manage to negotiate the same stretch of road every week without feeling the compulsion to slam into and knock down the acorn tree that has stood there for a hundred years.

POWER: Section 165 of The Road Traffic Act 1988 grants uniformed constables the power to seize any vehicles that are/were being driven on a public road without valid insurance or driving licenses. If other driving offences come to light (such as no MOT, bald tyres, seatbelts not worn, lighting faults, etc.) then officers may issue a Fixed Penalty Notice (fine and maybe points) or report the driver for process and a court appearance where a magistrate will hand down a suitable punishment.

Once the driver's details are acquired, their version of events briefly documented, and it is confirmed everyone has the required insurances and driving licenses, the priority turns to getting the road open as quickly as possible. Even for a short period a blocked road – especially at peak times – affects hundreds, or even thousands, of drivers and businesses, as well potentially having a knock-on effect for thousands more. Sub-contracted recovery firms will come out and remove any undriveable wrecks.

Once the mangled metal is removed, the slippery

vehicle fluids soaked up and traffic is freely flowing again, it is time to decide who's caused the collision and if they need points on their license and a potential court appearance to re-focus their mind and driving skills in the future. If an officer feels there is more than just an honest misjudgement behind an accident, a recommendation can be made to the force's 'Collision Administration Department' that further action should be taken against a driver. If they deem a prosecution is viable, they will take the necessary litigation steps.

Police do not however apportion blame with regards to who is at fault for insurance reasons – that's for the motorists involved as well as Tesco and Direct Line to squabble over.

As Seen on TV

The real masters of Roads Policing are ... traffic officers – unsurprisingly – with all the specialist crime fighting vehicles at their disposal. Traffic officers are easily identifiable because as well as driving larger saloon cars (sometime unmarked), they also traditionally wear flat caps with a white top (unlike the black topped variety warn by all other officers). When not attending serious RTC's and 'persecuting innocent motorists' (as the general public often accuse them of), traffic officers are out taking away the roads from criminals. Real criminals – not petty thieves like Geoff Steeles and the entire Butcher household – use the highways to travel and commit their dastardly deeds daily, and taking away that privilege handicaps them severely so is a high priority.

Traffic officers have many cool strategies and tools at their disposal for this purpose, but arguably the most valuable is the 'Automatic Number Plate Recognition' (ANPR) hardware installed in their high-powered interceptor vehicles. Capable of scanning five car number plates every second, ANPR can instantly advise officers of any vehicle without insurance, or with information markers if suspected to be involved in any suspicious activities, as well as if the vehicle in question is likely to be ferrying any nefarious, undesirable characters. The police have access to more than 10,000 operating ANPR cameras in the UK (many at fixed roadside locations) capturing circa 14 million images a year to a national database.

FACT: Traditionally traffic officers from the Metropolitan Police were referred to as the 'Black Rats' and would sometimes display a rat logo on both their police and personal cars to identify themselves to one another. The origin of this term is unclear; some have said that it is because traffic officers are like the rodent 'Rattus Rattus' and would eat their own – i.e. ticket their own family. A slightly more favourable explanation is that in days gone by their cars would return after a hard shift on the road covered in black grime.

"I've Only Had 2 Pints"

Something all police officers love, but especially those of the traffic persuasion, is to catch drivers 'over the prescribed limit' (OPL) for alcohol – drink drivers to the layman.

Drink driving is in many ways a classless crime: many everyday people would never dream of stealing from a shop, defrauding a business, or getting into a punch-up with a stranger, but they are prepared to take a chance on driving home when they know they might have had one too many. Business people, nurses, teachers, grandparents, pilots, members of the clergy and, dare I say it, the occasional police officer – all have been through the one-way steel custody gates having been caught doing just that before being instructed to blow into a white plastic tube at the roadside. Every driver involved in an RTC should be routinely breathalysed even if there is no immediate suspicion they may have been drinking.

FACT: It is estimated that 3,000 a year are killed or seriously injured in drink-driving accidents. Nearly one in six of all deaths on UK roads involve drivers over the legal alcohol limit. On average police conduct half a million breath tests every year and 100,000 are found to be positive.

Should a member of the public provide a positive specimen of breath (fail a breathalyser) at the roadside, they will immediately be arrested on suspicion of drink-driving and verbally cautioned. They will then promptly be transported to the nearest police station with facilities to conduct the police station breath procedure.

The detained person will next be invited to provide a further two specimens of breath on a much larger and more accurate machine. If they again blow over the limit on both specimens they will be charged with driving whilst over the proscribed limit and almost certainly be banned from driving and fined at court.

FACT: The legal drink drive limit cannot be safely converted into a certain number of drinks (and therefore units), as it depends on a number of factors that include gender, body mass and how quickly your body absorbs alcohol into the blood stream. The legal limit in the UK is 35 micrograms of alcohol in 100 millilitres of breath; or 80 milligrams of alcohol per 100 millilitres of blood; or 107 milligrams of alcohol per 100 millilitres of urine.

Should the driver fail by a slim margin they can then elect to have a blood or urine sample taken as well for analysis and comparison; however the likelihood of a different outcome is small. Failure by the member of the public to comply with proving a roadside specimen will result in instant arrest and a trip to the nick to provide samples on the station machine. Failure again to acquiesce will result in a charge of 'failing to provide' a breath specimen and also an inevitable ban and fine, so there is no escape. In circumstances of extreme medical conditions a suspect can instead conduct the test via the same blood or urine sample as mentioned above rather than blowing into a machine.

Drink-driving ruins careers, relationships and lives in an instant so is rightly punished hard.

14. Domestic Violence 101

Time for another definition (this time proudly brought to you by the Association of Chief Police Officers):

Any incident of threatening behaviour, violence or abuse (psychological, physical, sexual, financial or emotional) between adults (over eighteen) who are or have been intimate partners or family members, regardless of gender or sexuality.

"Any unit free to take a domestic?"

Thousands of officers every day up and down the country hear the above words spoken over their radios. It's Sunday evening and those are the words PC Knightly and I hear as we patrol the Chavington Manor estate.

"Repeat: any unit free to take a domestic at thirteen Mountpleasant Place, over?" the radio crackles again.

PC Knightly looks over to me from the driver's seat and rolls her eyes as we both know where we're off to next. This will be the third domestic we have attended already this evening. Sunday night is always domestic night. I assume it's because couples have been cooped up together all weekend with only each other's company and *X-Factor/Britain's Got Talent/Strictly Come Dancing/I'm a Celebrity/Big Brother* or heaven forbid - *TOWIE* (that's *The Only Way Is Essex* for the uneducated!) etc. as a distraction – dependent on the time of year and TV listings.

The very sight of Bruce Forsyth in a tuxedo is enough to make any normal, law-abiding, functioning member of society launch themselves into an uncontrollable rage aimed at their loved ones; why the very thought of Simon Cowell's smug and smarmy little face grinning back at me from my humble LCD TV makes me want to kick the cat right now* - I can only imagine the horror of seeing him in all his egotistical, high definition glory on a TV the size of the Butchers' one! The TV production companies have a lot to answer for as it is no surprise that with such limited entertainment at their disposal fully grown adults have no alternative but to resort to shouting obscenities at each other, throwing crockery and assaulting one another before calling the police to sort to out their wretched lives.

And trust me they do call – over and over again. Your common, lesser-striped police constable attends more domestic incidents than any other type of job.

Please note, abuse of domestic pets is a genuine risk factor to be considered when assessing a domestic violence threat and should not be condoned, trivialised, or be a source of humour, sarcasm or satire. I apologise unreservedly.

The Chavington Manor estate is made up of mostly social housing and full of salt-of-the-earth, hardworking and honest families. Sadly these citizens, whilst trying to go about their everyday lives, are overshadowed by a noisy minority who bring crime, antisocial behaviour and disorder, as well as a bad reputation to the area. Thirteen Mountpleasant Place is a well-known address to all police officers working the town Knightly and I do as we all frequently visit. It's where Sharon Peters lives with her brood of children and occasional on/off partner Wayne. You may recall Wayne 'Nature's Greatest Mistake' Butcher from a previous chapter.

As we are only just around the corner - and as our other busy colleagues must be unable to oblige - I press my radio button and acknowledge we can attend whilst also requesting the details.

The radio controller passes the following:

"We had a call from a neighbour. They say Sharon and her partner, a Wayne Butcher, is at the address and both are drunk. The informant says he's smashing up the place and they think he has hit her. Butcher is described as 'IC1', over six feet tall, stocky build, black polo shirt, blue jeans. Over."

PC Knightly fires up the blue lights and siren without hesitation.

There are two female officers on my team of which Knightly is one. With her diminutive physique and attractive looks, many deviant members of the public have underestimated her at their peril as she slaps the cuffs on them; for what she lacks in physical strength, PC Knightly more than makes up for with courage, initiative, dedication and wit.

On the short race to the end-terrace, three-bed property, the radio controller passes further information that in truth we already know:

There is a marker on the address stating Sharon is at high risk for domestic violence from Wayne, children are living at the address, and finally that all calls are to be treated as urgent (hence the pretty blue flashing lights we are bathing the estate in).

The controller also passes Wayne's PNC information:

"He has markers for VIOLENCE, ASSAULTS POLICE, DRUGS and ESCAPER. Wayne also has bail conditions to observe an 8pm to 7am curfew at another address (it is 2230hrs (10:30pm) so he is already in breach of that)," the controller continues, "PNC also shows he has a tattoo of a bulldog on his right forearm, and 'Mum' tattooed on his left shoulder. Over."

Killing the sirens a short distance away, Knightly and I pull up outside the house. Raised voices and colourful language can be heard within. I run to the front door and knock loudly, shouting in my most menacing police voice:

"Open up, it's the police!"

PC Knightly takes hold of the handle, turns it, and opens the door instead (told you she was bright). A Staffordshire bull terrier darts out the opening and disappears into the night before either of us can react. We both cautiously enter and are greeted by the sight of several smashed plates on cheap looking laminate flooring with huge gaps between the planks and skirting (people of Sharon and Wayne's calibre always have poor décor taste and terrible DIY skills – fact). Why crockery is always the missile of choice in domestic arguments I do not know.

There is the familiar smell of cannabis in the air. Sitting on the stairs are two younger sobbing children and a sadly accustomed 10-year-old who points to the living room on the right and says:

"He's hit my mum again. They're in there."

"Thanks Kane, you all OK though?" I reply. "Do you three want to go upstairs please?"

They saunter off. The children have been seen and appear unharmed, which is one of the things officers attending domestics must ensure.

We enter the garishly pink painted living room and both Wayne and Sharon turn and shout in harmony:

"What the **** do you want?!" (This is a fairly standard greeting to Justice Crusaders like us on the estate.)

"We've had a call to say there's been an argument," explains my colleague.

"I bet it was that nosey b*tch next door, innit!" snorts Sharon. She is right, but we won't be telling her that.

Sharon is a mostly single mother in her mid-twenties. Today she sports a pink Playboy vest top, pink jogging bottoms and white trainers. Her dark hair is scraped back into a pony tail making the egg-shaped lump on her forehead very noticeable. Her neckline and fingers are adorned with scroat standard-issue chunky gold jewelry and her ears feature large hooped rings. A non-standard addition is the Alphabetti Spaghetti in tomato sauce stuck in Sharon's hair.

"It doesn't matter who called us," PC Knightly interjects, "what's happened?"

"Nothin'. We don't need ya," replies Wayne on his lover's behalf.

"Wayne, come outside and talk to me," I suggest.

Wayne shakes his head, rolls his eyes, but steps over the broken coffee table to speak with me in the front garden. Getting the two warring parties separated as quickly as possible is an ideal start in diffusing conflict.

If I was asked by the Home Secretary my views on how to address the financial deficit and crisis threatening police budgets, my first suggestion would be to cull the entire Butcher bloodline. This would save the police, government and taxpayer alike tens of thousands of pounds a year. If this proposal was deemed too drastic and rejected, a reasonable compromise would be to at the very minimum to sterilise all the Butcher males to prevent the future fruit of their loins infecting the world further.

Wayne is 6'2" and 15 stone of mostly stocky build, yet also rotund around his gut. His matted, receding hair is particularly greasy today. He obviously came over this evening with the intention of wooing Sharon in to love-making as he is wearing pungent, overpowering aftershave and his best knock-off Ralph Lauren brand polo shirt and jeans that are normally reserved almost exclusively for court appearances.

"So Wayne, talk to me, what's been going on?"

"Huh? Are you new?" mumbles the hulk.

"No, Wayne, I'm not." I've met, and arrested, Wayne several times before. "So what's been going on tonight with you and Sharon?"

He spits on the floor before lighting a roll-up. "She's been drinking again, ain't she?" Wayne himself smells like he has just fallen in to a vat of special brew. "I just came over to see my son. He's not been well and I've been a bit worried about him," the father-of-the-year candidate continues, "so I get here, and she just goes spastic at me as soon as I get in the house, blood! Trying to hit me and stuff. I don't want to press charges of assault though. I'll just be off back to mine, yeah?"

Nice try. "Hang on a sec Wayne, the other officer is talking to Sharon. Let's wait and see what she has to say first."

After another spit: "Oh yeah, that officer is well fit, I remember her." Wayne nudges my elbow and winks suggestively inviting me to agree. "I wouldn't mind her arresting me! Huh?"

I'm sure my crewmate will be not-so-delighted to know her feminine charms have cast a spell on the

Neanderthal before me. Why Sharon (or indeed any female with even the lowest of standards) would allow fornication with Wayne is beyond me, but he clearly sees himself as somewhat of a ladies' man.

"So how have you been since you got out?" I ask as this is the first time I have encountered Wayne since his most recent release back into society having not been rehabilitated in prison.

"Yeah, alright. I'm staying out of trouble." (I could point out to him this is clearly not true as he has already acquired some bail conditions, but I won't.) "I'm keeping my 'ead down now," is the highly disputable and rehearsed return.

I already suspect that it is Sharon who should have kept her head down when Wayne threw whatever it was that has left its mark on her.

"Where's Tiger? Have you seen my dog?" asks Wayne, looking around at the open door, presumably for the mutt that made a sharp exit upon our arrival.

"Erm, so you're staying out of trouble you say..." quickly deflecting the question.

"Dat's a pedigree dog, ya' know, cost me 300 quid."

I'm really not interested in small talk with Wayne – in truth we don't have much in common and move in a different circle of friends. I am however interested in keeping Wayne talking whilst PC Knightly speaks with his marginally better half in the living room about the head injury she has acquired.

Away from the prying ears of Wayne and I – unaware of the sexual appeal she holds for Mr Butcher – PC Knightly puts her communication skills to good use.

"What's happened tonight, Sharon?"

"None of your business, I don't need ya, get out of my yard (or house)."

"Something's obviously happened; the house (or yard) is all smashed up."

As emotion overcomes her a tear runs down Sharon's left cheek, whilst at the same time a spaghetti hoop runs down the right one.

"Well it was him of course. We'd split up – for good this time – but he invited himself round, we had a few drinks together, it was nice, yeah?"

"Go on..." prompts Knightly.

"Then as usual he starts asking who I was seeing whilst he was inside and it all turns nasty, he threw a plate of food over me, and ..." Sharon points to her egg head.

"Do you want an ambulance to take a look at that?"

"No, no, it's fine. I just feel a bit dizzy, innit."

"I'll call one anyway, just to be on the safe side. They probably already have a few in the estate anyway at this time of night."

Knightly calls up on her radio to make the request for a paramedic before continuing:

"So what did he hit you with?"

"The *Sex In The City* Complete Box Set: Special Edition." Sharon now points to Wayne's weapon of choice, lying on the grubby rug next to a small empty drugs bag with a cannabis leaf image printed on it.

"That *must* have hurt," empathises Knightly.

"Yeah, it's on 12 discs. Wayne got it for me for my birthday yesterday." PC Knightly immediately suspects the local HMV's next stock-take will reveal an unpaid-for copy is AWOL from their shelves.

"I don't want him arrested though, I love him!" She pauses to take another pull on the roll-up she's smoking. "And his family will be up here giving me grief if he gets nicked, innit! And I've had enough of the 'Social' getting involved with the kids, mate!"

Fortunately for Sharon, although she doesn't realise it yet, the decision as to whether her beloved is arrested is now out of her hands: Sharon has disclosed to a police officer that a crime (namely an assault – nay, a *domestic-assault*) has taken place, and there is evidence in the house to support that – signs of a disturbance, not to mention that rapidly swelling, greasy forehead of hers. If Wayne was not arrested, this would imply that it is acceptable to physically abuse Sharon, and he would continue to do so until one night when he gets really drunk and seriously injures her (or worse).

Time for those much anticipated and impactive domestic violence statistics I promised; I know that you have been looking forward to them:

FACT: Every minute police in the UK receive a domestic assistance call – yet only 35% of domestic violence incidents are reported to the police.

Two women a week are killed by a current or former male partner according to Home Office figures.

Domestic violence has a higher rate of repeat victimisation than any other crime. On average, a woman is assaulted 35 times before her first call to the police.

The 2001/02 British Crime Survey (BCS) found that there were an estimated 635,000 incidents of domestic violence in England and Wales. 81% of the victims were women and 19% were men.

For the reasons above, domestic violence is taken *very* seriously by the police, and front-line PC's like Knightly and I know the grave consequences – both from a professional point of view, as well as an humanitarian one – if domestic violence perpetrators are not robustly dealt with. Nothing has more potential to come back and bite an officer on the backside than a poorly handled domestic that later turns into a serious assault – or worse, murder – when officers have left. To emphasize this fact there are more posters about the subject on the walls around the police station than there are Justin Bieber ones in a teenage girl's bedroom. Many police officers have lost jobs over not adhering to standard operating procedures when the worst has then happened. But, as long as an officer has done all they can, offered as much help to the victim as possible, and recorded and passed on all the relevant information, no one can criticise when things go bad.

With Wayne's fate already decided but neither him nor Sharon yet aware, things now become a bit awkward; PC Knightly knows all hell will break loose if the cuffs go straight on Wayne, so some diplomacy must be introduced.

"I know you don't want him arrested, but it can't keep going on like this, can it?"

"Yeah, but, no, but, he's nice when he's not drunk and on drugs," Sharon insists, but presents a poor argument.

"What happens if the next time something worse happens and he really hurts you?" Knightly presses on regardless.

"He wouldn't do that. I don't think so anyway. I love him, plus he's so good in bed." An officer with less fortitude than Knightly probably would have vomited in their mouths a little at that thought. "I just want us to be a happy family, we love our kids, innit!"

"Mummy, can I have some more cola?" squeaks a little voice from the hallway.

"Beyonce, get back to bed!" screams Mum. The infant bursts in to tears and scampers back upstairs.

Resigned to the fact Knightly isn't going to convince Sharon there are plenty more fish in the sea, she gets back to the task at hand.

"Sharon, I've got to ask you some questions for a domestic violence risk assessment."

"Oh not again! They're the same answers as I gave that copper three days ago!"

Regardless, Knightly asks Sharon about two dozen strategic questions about her relationship with Wayne and the children in the house. Sharon will be asked about past violent incidents, any threats to kill her or himself, if Wayne has access to weapons (in particular knives or firearms), use of drugs or alcohol by them both, any financial problems, examples of social isolation and possessive and/or controlling behaviour, not to mention the all-important abuse of family pets query! In recent years, additional risk-factor questions have been added about honour-based violence which is more common in ethnic minority cultures. Honour attacks are punishments on people, usually (but not exclusively) on women, for acts deemed to have brought shame on a family. Around 3,000 of these incidents were reported to police in 2011 but many more go unreported.

Before going off-duty Knightly or I will prepare a report to be perused by a supervisor and, if required (which in this case it definitely will be), referred to a specialist police domestic violence team.

"Sharon I want you to give me a statement about what you've just told me. Is that ok?" A rhetorical question if ever I heard one.

"No way! I told you, I don't want him nicked," Sharon is defiant.

Knightly perseveres: "Ok, but instead can I take some photos of your injuries?"

Knightly knows the answer to this one too: "Nah, sorry, he'll go mad if I do!"

Instead Knightly gets Sharon to sign her pocket notebook stating she does not wish to make a complaint, will not support a police prosecution or assist in any way, and that she makes that decision of her own free will.

TOP TIP: If you remember the 'Four P's' that a knowledgeable (but slightly sexist) old sweat of an officer once shared with me, the first was 'Pocket Notebook'. Asking reluctant victims to sign a 'PNB' stating they do not wish to make a complaint is as much about the officer protecting themselves as it is about anything else. Members of the public are sometimes a fickle bunch and can tell lies! At a later date they may complain that it was the police officer in attendance that did not take them seriously or want to take a statement. If the officer's notebook bares the deviant victim's signature, it is much harder for them to argue this point. Also, to aid with recollection at a later date, note down any injuries seen, or any sights you witnessed that suggest a crime has taken place.

The ever endeavouring Knightly has done all she can at the scene for Sharon and right on cue the ambulance arrives to check her over just as she sparks up her fifth cigarette since police arrival. Whilst Sharon is distracted, PC Knightly uses great stealth to appropriate and evidentially seize the 'weapon of offence' (the DVD box set) and conceals it in her paperwork bag so that there is at least some evidence to put to Wayne in interview.

POWER: Under Section 19 of the Police And Criminal Evidence (PACE) Act 1984, a police officer, whilst lawfully on any premises, can seize any item as long as there is reasonable grounds to believe that item has been obtained during the commission of crime, or it is evidence in relation to the investigation of any offence, or if it is necessary to seize said item to prevent the loss of evidence.

Meanwhile outside – in between spitting on the floor so much that when combined with his alcohol drinking I'm surprised he hasn't succumb to dehydration – Wayne continues to enthral me with his wit and wisdom.

Whilst swaying with intoxication: "I wanted to become a police officer when I went to school you know ... but I was too intelligent! Ha ha! Just kidding, mate, you're all right."

"Very funny Wayne," my eyes roll. "So are you working at the moment?"

"Ha! Nice one, copper. You're funny too." I guess I am.

Wayne will probably never do an honest day's work in his life, but then, as he inarticulately says: "Why should I get a job? I've got everythin' I need, innit."

A sad truth spoken by a true member of the 'Unworking Class' that plagues this country. Until a government finally makes good on their usual pre-election promise to reform the benefits system, people like Wayne will continue to leach off society, supplementing the ample job seekers allowance they already receive with petty crime to sustain their meagre existence.

Thankfully, before Wayne continues with his stand-up routine, Knightly joins us outside. Wayne sucks in his stomach, stands up straight and sticks out his chin as she approaches, in a pathetic attempt to look debonair.

"Wayne, I've been speaking to Sharon: you're going to have to come down the police station with us."

Here comes the awkward bit.

"What!? I ain't done nothing! She assaulted me! You're joking right?"

"I'm not, Wayne. Put your hands out," Knightly instructs Wayne as she removes her handcuffs from her stab vest. I take hold of Wayne's wrist but he twists his arm and pulls away.

"Well I'm gonna run if you try to arrest me," says Wayne, taking a step away from us.

"Well we'll chase you then," I say.

"OK," says Wayne.

"OK," says I.

The three of us now stand perfectly still waiting for one of the others to make the first move. My finger hovers over the emergency button on my radio just in case. Wayne is a big lump; his 'VIOLENT' marker is well justified, and when he decides to kick off it usually involves rolling around the floor with several police officers, arms and legs everywhere, like playing some sort of brutal game of Twister.

Should Wayne indeed run and/or fight, I am fully prepared: my strict fitness regime of eating only junk food at all times of day and night for four shifts a week, coupled with every few months completing the first two weeks of the P90X workout video series before losing motivation again, will stand me in good stead I am sure!

I would mention at this juncture that should (even after finishing this book) you still have desires to one day be an officer of the law, you will from time to time be assaulted. Just like Wayne having to accept being arrested every so often as a result of his criminal career path choice, being assaulted is an occupational hazard for police officers. To soften the blow (literally) officers are provided with specialist training and equipment, and in most cases assaults on officers are only minor ones. Plus if you do get assaulted and the culprit is charged, you might even get a little compensation money awarded your way at court!

"Oh! What's the point?" Wayne throws his arms up in the air like a petulant child before bringing them back down again and offering his wrists to Knightly who doesn't need a second invitation and quickly snaps on the cuffs.

"Oi! What you doing!? Let him go you *******s!" screams Sharon from the threshold of the house.

"Quick, get him to the car!" I suggest, tugging Wayne in the direction of our panda.

I hastily search Wayne for any weapons of mass destruction (or at least any implement he might injure me, my colleague or himself with) before pushing him into the back seat and sitting next to him as Knightly speeds us away, just before Sharon can reach us. On the way to the station, this being the soonest practicable time to do so, Knightly formally arrests and verbally

185

cautions the detainee. Wayne's reply to the caution is a loud burp which fills the panda with an unpleasant bouquet of stale lager. Knightly records the arrest details and eloquent reply in her pocket notebook back at the station.

POWER: A police constable will search a freshly arrested prisoner for any items which may cause harm to themselves or others, as well as anything which could aid their escape from custody. This power is afforded under Section 32 of the Police And Criminal Evidence Act 1984 (the same section which can also allow the search of premises upon arrest, but more on that later). It is paramount for safety reasons that an arresting officer is satisfied a prisoner is not in possession of any potentially harmful implements before transporting them to a police station.

Wayne is drunk so can't be interviewed until the morning. Back in custody he is searched more thoroughly and a small bag of cannabis is found in his sock. He is further arrested for possession of a Class B controlled drug. Wayne was also in breach of his curfew bail conditions so is further arrested for that too. He was also apparently identified by CCTV footage to be responsible for a theft of a DVD box set from a well-known High Street retailer the day before – again, further arrested. Finally, Wayne has an outstanding non-payment of fines warrant issued earlier that week by the local magistrates court (he'll be arrested for that after these other offences are dealt with). Wayne's had a bad night so I will wait until another time to break the news to him about Tiger as well. Instead he is bedded down for the night so Knightly and I can complete a handover package for the prisoner handling team to deal with him in the morning.

Because the victim, Sharon, was unhelpful and would provide no evidence, we have to complete statements detailing what unpleasantries we saw at the house (the scenes of a disturbance – not the horrible décor), what was said to us by the two protagonists and, in particular, the injuries on Sharon's head.

A referral will be made to the Domestic Violence Unit as Sharon is rightly considered 'High Risk' of serious injury in future incidents. They will contact Sharon and offer their services which she will decline (again). A second referral will be made to Social Services as Sharon's children should of course not be subjected to witnessing their mother being assaulted on a regular basis by her lover.

Knightly and I sign off for the night at 3 a.m. – just an hour late off – knowing that there was nothing more we could have done but, if sure of nothing else, we will be visiting thirteen Mountpleasant Place again soon.

The tale of woe that is Sharon and Wayne's is a typical one. Despite many of her problems being self-inflicted, Sharon is still a genuine victim and therefore police are duty bound to assist her as best as possible, irrespective of wanting to metaphorically pick her up and shake her vigorously for the poor relationship and lifestyle choices she continually makes. It is most likely Wayne will be interviewed in the morning, deny everything, before being released without charge as there will be insufficient evidence to prove he caused the injuries to Sharon without her cooperation and testimony. Even if he was charged, the likelihood of a successful conviction at court is minimal. Sharon will instead allow Wayne back into her life, home and bed. The cycle of abuse will continue until something breaks that chain; PC Knightly and I just hope it will not be the serious injury or even death of Sharon that does so.

15. Menace to Society

'Antisocial behaviour (ASB) is any aggressive, intimidating or destructive activity that damages or destroys another person's quality of life' – The Home Office.

ASB is a poisonous disease infecting many neighbourhoods and, if untreated, an epidemic threatens to spread across the whole country. There are many symptoms but very few effective antidotes and amputating the afflicted limb is not an option. As well as robustly policing the perpetrators of these low-level crimes and inconveniences, the police service is being increasingly asked to prevent re-offending, as well as vaccinate society from such occurrences ever happening again. In many ways this is unfair as the police are without the time, resources, expenses or equipment to undertake a challenge of such magnitude. The burden of curing such a serious affliction should fall upon the community as a whole but, as is often the case, when society falters the police are made the scapegoat as they have failed in their impossible duty of upholding the peace.

Tackling ASB is usually the remit of safer neighbourhood or local policing teams, but all front-line police officers have a responsibility to combat this scourge and will find themselves called into the fight. As mentioned previously, ASB is a sensitive and emotive issue to the taxpaying public; a constabulary's local reputation may hinge on how it deals with it and as such, ASB will be a 'force priority' and the police response must be 'victim focused' and 'engaging' (the police love these type of 'buzz phrases').

FACT: In 2010-11, the police in England and Wales recorded 3.3 million incidents of antisocial behaviour. But many other incidents are reported to other agencies, such as local councils and housing associations, or not reported at all.

The police fight ASB by conducting high visibility patrols in hot spot areas, and disperse any troublemakers – but this is where the problem lies: generally the authorities are only moving the problem on either temporarily, or just on to a whole new area to be blighted. Identifying specific offenders and then finding substantive offences for which to prosecute can be a difficult challenge, and even then the courts may not pass down serious enough punishments to deter them.

Often the same nuisance faces, who have no consideration for their fellow citizens, crop up time and again. Let me tell you a little about some of the more colourful characters that frequent our town.

ASBO, Innit!

The first is Samantha Trollchild. She is one of the 'Chicken Children' who worship at the altar of southern fried delights on the leisure park. As well as an unhealthy fondness for hanging around outside a certain fried chicken outlet, the Chicken Children also enjoy spitting, swearing, underage drinking, mopeds, as well as low hanging trousers and marijuana. Looking like they have been caught up in an explosion inside JJB Sports, casual sports clothing is the order of the day for this motley crew.

'Sammi' is aged 15, about 5'4" tall, obnoxious, recently had a controversial abortion, and is slightly overweight (no doubt 'The Colonel' has something to do with this). She lives with her reluctant mother in the Chavington Manor Estate and regularly comes to the attention of the police for various anti-social and misdemeanour offences. Her most recent brush with the law came about when upsetting rush-hour motorists on the high street.

As I arrive on the scene several youths deliberately distance themselves from a large half-drunk bottle of Lambrini now abandoned on the pavement.

"Look out, it's the Po-Po*!" is how I am greeted. Trollchild rolls her eyes, mutters something inaudible about bacon* and waddles over to me.

I open with, "Hello Samantha."

"I keep telling you copper, that does not be my name. I is called Sammi!"

She has a strange accent – think of a very loud, West Indian Vicky pollard. This is despite her pasty, freckly, Caucasian (or IC1 – more on that shortly) complexion and ginger hair.

Rather amusingly, in a desperate and unsuccessful attempt to beautify herself, Samantha appears to have recently shaven off her real eyebrows and drawn on thick black ones as replacements. These resemble two fighting caterpillars doing battle on her forehead and bring an instant smile to my face.

By coincidence, just last Saturday I arrested Samantha's mother for a public order offence on the very same high street her offspring now stands! Samantha doesn't know her father but has in the past proudly assured me he was black and as such always states her 'self-defined ethnicity' (SDE) to be 'mixed race – white/black Caribbean' or 'M1'.

Every time an individual is spoken to by the police – irrespective of whether they are victim, offender/suspect or witness – they are asked to choose their 'self-defined ethnicity' from a list of 16 options. (There is also a further option to decline, hence this Home Office recording method is referred to as 'SDE 16+1'.)

Asian or Asian British
    A1 – *Indian*
    A2 – *Pakistani*
    A3 – *Bangladeshi*
    A9 – *Any other Asian background*

Black or Black British
    B1 – *Caribbean*
    B2 – *African*
    B9 – *Any other Black background*

Mixed
    M1 – *White and Black Caribbean*
    M2 – *White and Black African*
    M3 – *White and Asian*
    M9 – *Any other Mixed background*

Chinese or other ethnic group
    O1 – *Chinese*
    O9 – *Any other ethnic group*

White
    W1 – *British*
    W2 – *Irish*
    W9 – *Any other White background*

    NS – Not Stated.

Strangely we ask individuals to pigeon-hole themselves into an ethnic category to prove we are *not* racist and treat everyone equally. This actually causes more offence and bewilderment to members of the public when the Home Office does not recognise their specific ethnic background and they are forced to choose categories such as 'white other', 'black other', or 'mixed race other'! I guess the Home Office doesn't do irony.

"Samantha, have you been mooning at passing cars?"

"What?! Is you a gay?" she squawks at me as her posse sniggers behind her. "You would like me to get my ass out, innit! Peado! I swear down on my dead baby's life that you is a batty-boy!"

Quite often the youth of today make no sense whatsoever when they talk.

"She ain't been doing nothing wrong, dude. What is it with the One-Time* in dis town?" chirps up one of Sammi's cronies.

"Well your clothing matches the description of a person reportedly doing just that."

"Well we is all dressed the same, innit, Five-O*!" Miss T eloquently informs me.

A point well made; Miss Trollchild and her crew are all clothed like they have corporate sponsorship from Adidas and other popular sports clothing manufacturers – I have seen fewer stripes at a police sergeant's promotion board than that which I am presented with right now! Maybe this is because although none of Sammi or her 'bredin' are athletes, they often find themselves running (away).

"Shall I ask the local CCTV operators to check their cameras and see if it was you?" I helpfully suggest.

"Whatever, policeman, it weren't me! Why is the Babylon* always up in my face, blood?"

"Oh I don't know, maybe because you keep doing ill-advised things like waving your derriere at passing motorists, Samantha?" I hint, losing patience a little with the kindergarten before me.

"What?"

"Your posterior, Samantha?" I try to elaborate.

"What?"

"Your backside!" I spell it out.

"What?!"

"Never mind." I give up.

Before leaving Samantha and her crew I run a quick PNC check on her via my Blackberry. Whilst conducting the check I am informed by an on-looking youth with a glazed-over expression on his face that my police Blackberry is the old model and as such 'seriously uncool'. Samantha is not wanted or in breach of her current ASBO (anti-social behaviour order) so I warn her one more time about her future conduct, before confiscating the alcohol and leaving the scene.

POWER: Section 29 of The Policing and Crime Act 2009 grants police officers and PCSOs the power to seize alcohol from people under the age of 18. It also grants officers the power to return children under the age of 16 who have been found with alcohol to their parents or a place of safety.

There is no doubt Sammi is a horrible little street urchin who will most likely continue to cause strife for the townsfolk and police alike for many years to come, but I do have sympathy for her. Having met Sammi's mother and seen her home it is not hard to see why she has so spectacularly gone off the rails. Is enough being done by her family, social services, the police or society to put her back on track? Probably not. I cannot change her past, but maybe as an authoritative figure I can influence her future. The police service has a responsibility to the troubled youth of today and the impact it can have should not be underestimated.

* *all street vernacular for 'Police' by the way.*

Use the force

Next up is Boris Kalashnikovski. A 36-year-old foreign national from a non-descript Eastern European country (to avoid any accusations of stereotyping), so his SDE 16+1 is 'W9 – white any other background'.

You might recall I mentioned a male who once passed the time of day trying to decapitate a pigeon with his bare teeth as dozens of mortified shoppers looked on? That would be Boris. In fairness to him, on that particular day he was not himself – he was highly plastered on a cocktail of drink and hallucinogenic drugs that would have rendered most human beings in a coma. Boris is a street drinker who just loves cheap cider – or any alcohol he can get his hands on for that matter – almost as much as he hates police officers. He is 6'2" tall and of willowy build – testimony to the mostly liquid diet he religiously upholds.

One fine summer afternoon, police are called to Dickens Park by members of the public complaining about a rowdy Eastern European male drinking, swearing, propositioning women and generally ruining the pleasant ambience.

The police use a simplified method of describing a person's ethnicity, referred to as 'IC codes'. ('IC' actually stands for 'Identity Code', so 'IC code' is technically a redundant acronym, but who ever said police talk was logical?) The codes are based on an officer's perceived view of an individual's ethnicity, as opposed to that of the individual's self-defined ethnicity (SDE 16+1). The codes are as follows:

IC1 – *White, northern European*

IC2 – *Mediterranean European/Hispanic*

IC3 – *Black, African/Afro-Caribbean*

IC4 – *Asian, Indian, Pakistani, Nepalese, Maldivian, Sri Lankan, Bangladeshi, or any other (South) Asian*

IC5 – *Oriental, Chinese, Japanese, or South-East Asian*

IC6 – *Arab*

The radio controller passes the suspect's description: "IC1 male, over 6 foot, slim build, seems intoxicated, wearing a grey t-shirt and dirty blue jeans."

PCSOs Chiverton and Okacha are already on the scene as I arrive, so all three of us take a stroll in the sunshine to find the public inconvenience. The PCSOs go one way whilst I go another to best search the vast park.

FACT: Police community support officers are members of support staff employed, directed and managed by their police force. They work to complement and support regular police officers, providing a visible and accessible uniformed presence to improve the quality of life in the community and offer greater public reassurance. Their powers include being able to issue fixed penalty notices for minor offences (e.g. littering, dog fouling, riding on footpaths), the power to confiscate alcohol and cigarettes, to demand the name and address of those acting antisocially, as well as to remove abandoned vehicles, to name just a few.

It is a truly beautiful day: the sun is shining, the birds are singing, the children are truanting. The bright sun is soothing as I stroll along (wishing I was not wearing a heavy stab vest) and people all around are enjoying the British summer time as they laugh and play in harmony. I nod and smile at the friendly civilians as I walk along with my head held high, enjoying the atmosphere.

The utopia is brought to a sudden and crashing end however when I find Boris urinating in a bush, with a can of super strength lager at his feet and his jeans around his knees. I am prepared to go out on a limb here and bet this is the male I am looking for.

"Boris, put that away, pull up your trousers, and come out of the bush please!"

"Wha... Who is youz, what youz want, eh?" Boris is a little confused and disorientated and appears to think the tree to his right is communicating with him.

(It is much more realistic – not to mention slightly funnier – if you read Boris's speech to yourself in a 'Borat' style accent. Please do not do this aloud though if you are on a busy train, bus or public place as we do not want to have to invoke the already discussed Section 136 of the Mental Health Act.)

"I'm PC Surname, Boris. Turn around and you'll see me," I suggest, already despairing at how this is going.

Boris slowly turns, pulling up his trousers and moving his head backwards and forwards as he squints, trying to focus on the tall, dark and handsome police officer now in front of him. He is clearly most intoxicated again and swaying rhythmically from side to side, trying to stay vertical. The crotch of his jeans is wet suggesting he did not quite make it to the bush in time.

After a short pause to find his bearings, Boris speaks. "Oh, mizter polizia man, yez? What youz want?"

"We've had some complaints about you causing problems in the park," I explain.

"Who, me? No, I no trouble mizter polizia man. I not know what you speak about," Boris plays the innocent with an unconvincing look of shock on his face.

"Someone complained that you were swearing at them and trying to start a fight."

"No, no, no! There was guy, but was nothing: seven to him, half of one dozen to me, yez? Officer, you join me for drink, yez? Come I have many more. Let us sit in sunshine, yez?"

As tempting as sharing a beverage with a smelly, drunk tramp with urine stains on his crotch is, duty must prevail and I thank Boris for his kind offer but respectfully decline his hospitality.

"Boris, you can't drink in the park, there are kids about. You're going to have to get your things together and move on."

"But why? I like park. I like trees. I like you, mizter polizia man! I be good boy and watch my Q's and P's, yez? Then I stay. No problemo!"

Boris tries to persuade me to let him stay but I think he is far too drunk for any good to come of him remaining where he is.

"No Boris, I'm afraid we still have a 'problemo'." I enter into diplomacy with my foreign friend. "Grab your things and I'll walk you out the park. If you promise not to spill any bodily fluids in my police car I might even give you a lift home."

I would much rather not have Boris in my police car as I will have his lingering stench everywhere I drive for the rest of the shift, but sometimes it's a sacrifice worth making – having to drive around with your windows open for a few hours – in the knowledge that at least Boris is several miles away from the good folk of the park.

It is obvious Boris is not impressed with my gracious offer but as he prepares to respond his concentration is broken as he spots a young woman walking behind me on the footpath.

"Well 'ello baby, how's you doin'?" Boris leers at the woman.

The girl turns to look at Boris, screws up her face, and tells him where to go in no uncertain terms (technically committing a minor public order offence of her own as she does, but we'll overlook that one) before she continues along the path.

Following his latest rebuttal Boris mutters something to himself in his native dialect before turning his attention back to me.

"Why I must go? I like park, has very nice trees. Youz just no like me, I thinks." Boris seems more impatient and determined now. "The birds, they are shining and the sun is singing, I not go. I think I stay here, yez? Maybe I go for swim in pond or have ice-cream."

"Boris, you're drunk, you're being disorderly, you're in a public place." I try my best to spell it out in a sterner tone. "You have to move on."

"I like Funny Feet lolly-pop, or maybe Feast ice cream. I like them both equally – is how you say: 'swings and seesaws' to me."

Momentarily I am a little taken aback: "Erm, that's nice Boris..."

"Not Magnum though, too expensive," he continues. "I think you are 99 cone with flake man, yez?"

I could go for a cone right now, but refocusing: "Boris, you have to go."

"Twister then?"

"No thanks."

"Choc-ice?"

"Boris! You have to leave the park!"

"No!" shouts a suddenly defiant Boris. The mood has quickly shifted and the atmosphere becomes tenser. "You go get your phaser gun, coz I not go!"

I haven't got one of those, and if I did I am in no doubt that disintegrating Boris into a pile of ash would be deemed 'excessive force' (I assume he means taser by the way). Boris has now adopted a side-on stance, shuffling his weight back and forwards he clenches and relaxes his fist repeatedly as he scans up and down my body as best he can with his boozy, wide, crossed eyes – all danger signs my training prepared me to look out for when a subject is becoming hostile. The four-letter swear words muttered under his breath by the increasingly angry Easter European are also clues of his shifting demeanour!

I call for another unit to join me via my radio as I can see where this encounter is quickly heading.

"Boris, calm down for me. There's no need to get angry," I try to defuse the situation.

"I think I fight youz. You go to hell, copper!" says Boris as he raises his fists up and circles them in front of himself like a comical Queensbury Rules pugilist of yesteryear.

My hands however are out in front, palms down, gesturing for Boris to relax a little. Inside my head though I am considering my options should Boris decide he wants to get up close and personal. There are many things to consider: Boris is taller and possibly stronger than me, he is drunk and unpredictable with a history of mental health issues, he could have a concealed weapon, I am in a public park in the middle of the day with members of the community all around whose safety I must also be mindful of. To my advantage I have my personal protective equipment available – my baton, incapacitant spray and handcuffs – not to mention Boris can barely stand. My two PCSO companions are still somewhere nearby in the park and other police officers are making their way to my location. All these are 'impact factors' or relevant and considered facts that I will later rely on to justify any use of force I utilize against Boris as he moves towards me menacingly.

"Spray, spray, spray!" I call out as a stream of incapacitant spray arcs out from my right hand and splashes all across Boris's ugly mug.

He grabs his face and starts to scream like a banshee as if his eyes are melting inside his head. Blood curdling Eastern European profanity fills the park as it spews forth from his mouth.

"Pava (the incapacitant spray) has been deployed, more units on the hurry up, please!" I excitedly shout down my radio so my colleagues know what has happened.

"Boris, drop to your knees," I instruct, "stop rubbing your eyes, it will make it worse!"

Boris crumples to the floor, still screaming loudly like the Wicked Witch of the West meeting her demise. I cautiously walk over, take out my handcuffs and place one half onto Boris' left wrist. As I try to apply the second cuff Boris pulls away, continuing to shout a tirade of abuse at me in his native tongue. The sudden movement causes me to fall over on top of Boris so we are now rolling around on the grass together like

Greco roman wrestlers but without the spandex. We are fighting.

"Boris, stop resisting, release your arm!" I bellow out, still trying to cuff him up. I'm sure Boris is shouting something offensive about my mother in reply but I can't be sure.

During my initial self-defence training, I was taught dozens of proven techniques to use in situations like this to gain control of subjects. Officers receive regular refresher training as well as updates in the latest and most effective pain compliance measures, pressure point manipulation, and also how to use an assailant's weight against them. Although not Chuck Norris, I am a moderately schooled and well-practiced semi-lethal weapon in mixed martial arts as a result of my police training, with various techniques at my disposal.

However, in this instance, as I roll around the ornamental garden of Dickens Park with a pungent Mister Kalashnikovski, I cannot remember any of my training. Instead, whilst still desperately trying to place the second cuff on Boris, the technique I choose to employ is not from the Personal Safety Training manual; at this time of trepidation I opt for a technique not technically Home Office approved at all – I go for the schoolyard classic 'Chinese burn'.

It is only whilst rolling around with Boris that his reeking funk truly becomes apparent. This man smells terrible! If we were in a cartoon there would be a green fog surrounding him right now and the flowers would be wilting around us.

After several minutes of struggling with each other, a certain someone's wrists now red raw, I finally win the war of attrition and lock up Boris. My nose is tingling and eyes stinging from the effects of the Pava after the roll around. We both have dirt on our faces, grass in our hair, and the seat of my trousers has ripped open showing my Super-Man novelty boxers (which I foolishly chose whilst in a rush to get ready having slightly overslept this morning) to the families standing nearby watching the festivities. To cap it all, I think I have also trodden in duck poo. The ever colloquial Boris might say we both look "like we has been pulled through bush in reverse, yez?"

As I lay on top of my prisoner – both of us breathing heavily and sweating – Smithy strolls around a nearby bush.

"What's going on here then?" Smithy enquires.

I am too tired and exhausted to answer, so instead just beckon over my colleague to drag off Boris. As he is lead away I muster enough strength to tell him he is under arrest for assaulting a police constable and a Section 5 public order offence (causing someone – namely me and the public – harassment, alarm and distress), before muttering something to him about not having to say anything, however going on to tell him it may harm his defence if he does not mention when questioned, something which he later relies on in court, and finally warning him everything he does say may be given in evidence (the police Caution).

All that is left for me to do is return to the station, write a detailed statement justifying my actions, complete a 'use of force' form further justifying my actions, complete another form to account for me discharging my incapacitant spray, before completing a handover package for when Boris is finally sober enough for interview. When all this is done I am in need of a shower and a new pair of trousers.

The episode with Boris demonstrates how so often even the simplest of sounding jobs – removing a drunken nuisance from a park – can turn out to have the most unusual of endings and why police officers always expect the unexpected. The variety and surprises which keep us on our toes are actually to many officers one of the most appealing perks of the job.

Dealing with ASB can be tedious but is ultimately a great way to serve the community and make a real impact in a local area, which is what all officers should take pride in as that is a primary aim of this job after all.

16. The Interweb

The World Wide Web is without doubt one of the greatest inventions of the twentieth century – uniting nations, bringing information and media to the masses, allowing instant communication across the globe, and in most cases making the world a better place. The police service benefits hugely from the internet and the information sharing it allows. *However*, it is also fair to say that no other innovation in recent time has caused more tribulation for police officers and put greater strain on police resources both locally and nationally.

Traditional crimes such as fraud and theft have been reinvigorated with the misuse of new online technologies. Some scams are elaborate and sophisticated, whilst others are simple and prey on the most gullible of victims – the astounding willingness of certain people to gleefully hand over cash or financial details to people they have never met for the promise of a future product or service, based purely on a glossy looking web page or enticingly worded email, never ceases to amaze.

The major complication and hindrance concerning the investigation of this type of crime is that very little tangible evidence is left and often offender and victim can be miles apart, spanning several police force borders; not to mention that many of the most popular web sites are American companies, so sometimes foreign law can also be a factor. Most forces now have specialist hi-tech crime departments dedicated to unravelling internet and auction site offences. As old cons are foiled, new and more adventurous ones are formulated by the crooks trying to stay one step ahead.

The only consolation to the ambushed victim is that as 'e-crime' has come to prominence, more banks and financial institutions – in an attempt to increase consumer confidence – now offer compensation to their often foolish customers so that the victim will get some, if not all, their money back. This is no comfort to the investigating police force however as, although the victim is recompensed and keen to put the whole sorry affair behind them, a crime has still taken place so a full investigation must ensue regardless (again resulting in lots of deceased trees) but now with a victim not that interested in giving up a few hours of their day to assist.

FACT: Cyber-crime costs the UK economy £27bn a year the government has said (February 2011). The brunt of this falls on businesses with £21bn of loss attributed to them. £2.2bn is the cost to the government and £3.1bn to the general public.

StalkBook.com

But no crime has benefitted more from the internet revolution than that of 'harassment'. There is one website that has cornered the market for this former niche pastime. Ask any police officer and they will tell you this particular web site is the tool of Satan (perhaps I'll ask Mad Mary to have a word then) and corrodes away countless police hours even when possibly no crime has actually yet taken place. In this wonderful modern age we live in, even the most under-educated simpleton can pick up his/her mobile phone or laptop and instantly abuse his/her former friend or lover from the comfort of their own home without missing an episode of *Eastenders* in the process. I am of course talking about Facebook!

As well as a revolutionary device by which to antagonize former friends, family and lovers, social networking is also a fantastically convenient way to publicize an imminent self-harming event. Nothing gets the 999 switchboard going like a poorly formulated status update:

"that is it. I had enuff. I is goin 2 end it. Laterz peeps..."

In the line of duty I've kicked in a person's door at the request of their loved ones for the sake of nothing more than a 'sad smiley' post on Twitter! Usually we find it was just a cry for help/attention from the sad Tweeter who is found alive and well, albeit a bit depressed, having usually just suffered a relationship drama. Still, their online activity got them the spotlight they craved (#attentionseeker).

Ironically – clearly unable to beat them – my police force has joined the social network revolution and has its own Facebook page. Here police officers and staff can appeal for witnesses to crimes, update members of the community about the goings on in their neighbourhoods, and of course invite citizens to give constructive feedback. A potentially fantastic tool to communicate with the masses you might think?

No.

Instead members of the public generally choose to use this forum to vent their frustrations at what they feel is the inept service we provide them and moan about the noisy police helicopter hovering above their house in the early hours of the morning – usually in 'txt' language too! The force's 'FaceBook fans' are usually chomping at the bit to offer some unconstructive advice and are always keen to tell us where we are going wrong!

TOP TIP: If a police officer is so inclined to have their own Facebook page, they should consider carefully what information regarding their employment and employer they display. Pictures in full uniform are never advisable; pictures in a state of undress and partial uniform is career suicide (trust me, officers have done it)! Even if only closest friends and family can view your profile, knowing the unique position in society you hold they may be tempted to ask small favours or for assistance that could, should you oblige, potentially and unwittingly place you in a compromised position with your employer. On that note: please check out the 'I Pay Your Wages' page on FaceBook where I can guarantee you will find no partial nudity whatsoever!

www.facebook.com/pcsurname

Malicious Communications

My police force, like many others, has adopted an appointment system for poor members of the public who have been the victims of crime to see a real life police officer in all their uniformed glory, so that they might complain in person about the injustices inflicted upon them. Suitable crimes for appointments are non-urgent ones that do not require an immediate call-out of a police officer as no imminent threat is posed to the target, but are however bona fide crimes with genuine upset victims and so require a police officer-to-victim personal consultation.

In my force this public relation exercise is called 'the appointment car' and is piloted by the 'appointment officer'. My colleagues and I have another much more appropriate name for this often tedious occupation but I will not share that with you.

By some unfortunate and cruel twist of fate I am that appointment officer today. My 1125hrs is to see Ian Sharlatun-Jones. The idea is that the appointment officer will travel to the member of the public's house at a time and date convenient to them, thus making the police force they represent appear friendly, accommodating and outreaching to the community. Strangely on this occasion the 'customer' has instead chosen to come to me at the police station for some as yet unknown reason. The setting for this encounter is a small, private room at the front of the police station where statements are generally taken.

Waiting for me is a tense-looking, middle class gentlemen, aged in his mid-thirties, dressed in a rather fetching tank top and collared shirt ensemble.

"Mr Sharlatun-Jones, I am PC Surname. Nice to meet you, please have a seat."

"Thank you," is the well-spoken reply.

With the pleasantries over, it is straight down to business as I have two other appointments after this one.

"So, what can we do for you today?"

I already have a brief outline of Mr Sharlatun-Jones's predicament as the call handler who books the appointments provides me with a brief resumé of the matter.

The gentleman sitting opposite me claims he is being harassed via the internet by a female named

Candy Green. This is a prime example of many of the assignments created for the appointment car.

"Well, you see, I was courting a girl called Candy, we only went out a few times about six months ago, but now she won't leave me alone!" Mr Sharlatun-Jones nervously rubs his hands together as he explains.

"I see. Carry on..."

"Well it has to stop! You need to stop her! It's a real problem for me, officer."

"How did you meet Candy?"

I already know it was via the internet as I said before, but I am making him tell me in his own words as I do not want to influence his account about what has happened to end him up in a police station. I do this in part because with open questioning (just like when interviewing suspects) he is more likely to elaborate further on the information he has already given over the phone; and also partly because I find it more fun this way.

"Well we met over the internet you see."

"I see..."

"On a website,"

"On a website, uh huh..."

"A certain type of web site..." a tentative and awkward Mr Sharlatun-Jones gestures his hand in a circular motion in front of him whilst nodding his head, clearly inviting me to finish his explanation for him.

Pretending to look puzzled and shaking my head: "OK...?" I am enjoying myself.

"A dating website, PC Surname!" he eventually blurts out.

"Ah, yes. Please carry one."

"We got in contact, sent a few emails back and forth before agreeing to meet. As I said we dated a few times but I called it off as it didn't seem to be going anywhere. Ever since she's been bombarding me with texts and emails."

"What website is this, please?" as I take out my pen to make some notes.

Mr Sharlatun-Jones hesitates before answering. "It's called FlirtyAndThirtyPlus.com.uk"

I raise an eyebrow and write the web address down. I may have to research that web site later – purely for professional and investigative reasons of course.

"So when did you last see Candy?"

"About three months ago. That was when I told her the relationship was off."

"And how often has she contacted you since?" I query.

"Nearly every day! This is why it must end now!" explains a worked-up Mr Sharlatun-Jones.

I continue to fact find. "What sort of things does she say in these texts and emails, Mr Sharlatun-Jones?"

"Well at first she just kept saying how much she loved me, and how she wanted to see me. When I stopped replying she became abusive and started making ... certain threats."

"Threats you say?" I put my best puzzled face on again.

"Yes, threats. She said... she said... she would put pictures up on her Facebook site of me and send those same pictures to my family."

Ah, of course! FaceBook strikes again! Who saw that coming?

211

"What sort of pictures?"

After another distinct hesitation: "Pictures of a revealing nature, PC Surname. Pictures of me."

"I see. How did she get these pictures, Mr Sharlatun-Jones?"

"Well, it's rather embarrassing: I may have sent them to her." Mr Sharlatun-Jones, with crimson cheeks, mumbled the last part of that sentence, but I won't make him repeat it out of courtesy because I am an understanding and respectful officer.

Mr Sharlatun-Jones hands me a printout of emails sent which I scan-read through.

"Who is PoshTotty96?"

"That's Candy's screen name."

"I see, so SexyBigBoy37 is...."

"Yes, that is me." He dips his head in a combination of shame and embarrassment.

"I understand and respect your predicament," I interject to break the awkwardness. "How seriously do you take these threats?"

"If she was to send those photos to certain family there would be grave consequences for my personal life, not to mention my professional one," explains the gentleman in a clearly concerned tone. "She knows this so I take it very seriously indeed."

As we have discussed before in the chapter about theft, there are certain 'points to prove' before a police officer will concede a crime has taken place and therefore an investigation should ensue which inevitably commences with a handwritten statement from the victim. In harassment cases those points are that the offender knows their actions are indeed causing the victim distress, that the offender knew their actions were likely to cause distress, and finally that a 'course of conduct' has taken place. The latter point means there must be more than one incident and some consistency in the abuse (that's not to say that an isolated incident is not necessarily an offence, but it does not constitute the heinous crime of harassment).

Having satisfied myself that the more than just mischievous Miss Green has been asked to cease contacting her former lover, that her continued refusal to do so is causing her target distress and also that – having read the several pages of printed emails Mr Sharlatun-Jones has just presented me – there is indeed a sufficient course of conduct, I have reached a conclusion based on the evidence I have before me: a crime has probably taken place! I am going to have to get my pen out and someone is going to get locked up, right? Not necessarily.

"So you would like Miss Green arrested, yes?" I ask.

"Heavens no! That will only make things worse! I was hoping instead you can speak with her and explain this must stop."

Peculiar creatures, members of the public: when there is no shred of evidence whatsoever that any crime has taken place they want their accused immediately plucked from thin air and locked up indefinitely without delay, and they will almost certainly make complaints against officers when their demands are not met. Yet when there *is* a crime, with compelling evidence to support it, *and* a named offender that can be easily located as well, then sometimes an arrest is the last thing they want!

As I hold the office of constable, I investigate crime and bring criminals to justice – it's my job. It is not my job to sort out awkward social inconveniences for people who use the internet for sexual gratification. But it is also my mission to prevent crime and as there is potential for this scenario to escalate into something far more serious should others become involved – not to mention that this is technically a 'domestic incident' open to scrutiny (see previous chapter) – I will indulge Mr Sharlatun-Jones and speak informally with Candy as he desires. Police officers regularly find themselves acting as agents and go-betweens for jilted lovers – much like that delightful Jeremy Kyle does, but with marginally less DNA testing.

Just as I wrap up proceedings my new client throws another ingredient into the melting pot.

"There is one other thing: Candy has a certain item of mine in her possession."

"Go on?" that puzzled look is back on my face, only this time it is for real as the plot thickens...

"A gold engagement ring. *My* gold engagement ring. I left it at her flat during a visit. She keeps offering to drop it back at my house but that would of course not be desirable."

Suddenly Mr Sharlatun-Jones's predicament along with his moral fibre starts to become much clearer.

"OK, I'll see what I can do. Shall I call you on your mobile after I have spoken with Miss Green?"

"No! Please don't do that. My fiancée has a few trust issues and I believe checks my messages. Besides, I don't want to cause her any stress – not in her condition – the baby is due in a couple of weeks. I will call you in a few days if that's OK."

And so I am posed with the ethical conundrum and dilemma that faces police officers across the land on a daily basis: having to balance necessary evils with higher purpose. Protectors of the Queen's peace are constantly torn between doing what's right and what the law dictates, as sometimes these two contradict each other. At these times, whenever possible, the devoted officer must be prepared, remain professional, uphold the law and endeavour to do their duties – even if that contravenes their personal opinion and code of conduct by which they live their own life. Although unscrupulous and ethically wrong, infidelity is not a criminal offence (otherwise many of my colleagues would be 'prolific and priority offenders') whereas harassment is. So I will still do Mr Sharlatun-Jones's bidding and speak with Miss Green.

After my other two appointments (one was with a woman who was reporting the theft of her prize winning tomato plants, and the other the gentleman evidently forgot I was coming and left me waiting outside his house for thirty minutes and wouldn't answer his phone so I left), I now have time to track down Miss Green and offer some words of advice.

I arrive at the address Mr Sharlatun-Jones has provided for his former associate. The modern-built, luxury block of flats towers high above me as I press the intercom button for Miss Green. A sultry female voice answers:

"Hello, is that Miss Green? It's PC Surname here from the police. Can I have a word please?"

"A police officer? Oh my, you'd better come up then."

I make my way up four flights of stairs, slightly out of breath and thinking it might be time to dig out my fitness DVD's once more, before knocking on the door of flat 4b. The door is opened by an attractive woman most likely aged in her late-forties but who looks much younger.

Taking me by surprise, Miss Green enquires in a husky voice not unlike Kathleen Turner off of the 1980's:

"You're not the stripper are you?"

"Huh? Pardon? No!"

"Shame," giggles Candy. "I'm only joking, darling. Please come in and tell me what I can do for you. Have I been a naughty girl?"

I enter. "Well, I've been speaking with a gentleman who has made an allegation that you've been harassing him," I say.

"You've been speaking with Dermot O'Leary?"

"What? No. Dermot O'Leary? No."

"Oh, then you have been speaking with Ian Sharlatun-Jones then," Miss Green rolls her eyes and walks into the living room, so I follow.

"Correct. What's been going on then?"

Often in situations like this there are two sides (or more) to every story and it is always worth keeping an open mind about any allegation until all parties involved are spoken to. Often the role of 'offender' and 'victim' is initially determined only by whoever called the police first until the full facts are established; once the true events are determined the offender and victim tags may be reassigned and reversed.

As before, I invite Miss Green to explain the whole situation in her own words before revealing what I already know. Instead she declines my invitation to tell her side of the story and chooses to try and flirt outrageously with me.

Completely ignoring my questioning: "Is that your truncheon I can see?" Candy's voice is full of playful innuendo as she wiggles her finger in the general direction of the baton protruding from my belt.

Remaining professional but ever so slightly blushing inside: "Miss Green. Please tell me about your relationship with Mr Sharlatun-Jones."

Miss Green rolls her eyes again before reluctantly answering me. "I met Ian via a dating web site. He's not my usual type if I'm honest but we went out a few times. After a few months of seeing each other he told me he loved me but suddenly revealed he had a pregnant fiancé stashed away somewhere."

Candy nonchalantly recounts her unlikely love story to me whilst examining her manicured painted nails the whole time.

"Carry on," I prompt.

"He told me he was going to leave her for me, sell his business, and we'd go travelling around the world together. After a few more weeks, I realized he clearly had no intention of leaving his betrothed so I called the whole thing off. He begged me to have him back and when I refused he became abusive. Now I'm not the kind of lady that will tolerate that."

"How long ago since you last contacted Mr Sharlatun-Jones?"

"Erm, what time is it now?"

"You've contacted him today?!"

"I may have sent him an email." Miss Green tilts her head down and flutters her eyelids, playfully looking for sympathy and forgiveness like a naughty school girl.

"Miss Green, this must stop. Mr Sharlatun does not wish to make a formal complaint at this time, but has asked me to advise you to cease any contact with him immediately as if this persists then it is likely you'll be arrested," I assertively explain.

"Oh, officer, you are so demanding," now wide-eyed Candy mischievously replies, clearly not taking my threats at all seriously. "You know I've heard them say police officers are getting younger, but I didn't know they were more handsome as well," she provocatively continues in her husky voice, changing the subject completely, slowly and suggestively moving towards me.

My stern façade cracks as I can't help but smile as I realize the lady is teasing me just as she has been the hapless Mr Sharlatun-Jones. I feel my cheeks flush red and think I remember why as an adolescent I always had a fondness for the repeats of *Jewel of The Nile* and *Romancing the Stone* on TV.

Realising a different and softer approach is required I go on. "Candy, I think you know what I'm saying. You've had your fun with Ian, *please* can you stop emailing, texting and toying with him anymore," I appeal, now with a wry grin.

Miss Green flashes a knowing smile at me. "OK, as much as I wouldn't mind being restrained in your handcuffs, you can tell Ian he won't hear from me again."

"Excellent. And you won't be putting any compromising pictures of him on FaceBook, right?"

Miss Green roars with laughter. "No, I promise. You wouldn't see much even if I did if you know what I mean, darling!" She raises her hand and bends out her wriggling little finger causing me to smirk.

"Thank you. Ah, whilst I remember, do you happen to know anything about his engagement ring?"

She reaches towards a shelf and hands the gold band to me which I place in my pocket for safekeeping.

"I'll make sure this is returned to him."

"Thank you. Tell him to be more careful with his possessions," before again Candy reverts to a suggestive tone once more. "Now, I see *you're* not wearing a ring though. You know I have my own handcuffs too. What time do you get off duty, PC Surname?"

With the words of advice from the training school PSD input ringing in my ears, as well as my career and pension flashing before my eyes, I beat a hasty retreat, excuse myself and leave the flat as quickly as I can before I'm eaten alive.

A day later Mr Sharlatun-Jones calls and I update him of my encounter with the flirtatious man-eater. He thanks me for my assistance and I tell him the property reference number to give to the property manager when he comes to the station to collect his ring. Another happy customer.

17. Public (dis)Order

When the police refer to 'public order' they are referring to any gathering of people in a public place where there is potential for the people to misbehave. This might be at a sports event, a protest (peaceful or otherwise), carnival, or even a full scale riot (although police forces rarely use the 'R' word as should such a spectacle take place within their jurisdiction then that particular force has failed in the task of controlling their citizens and maintaining peace; as such they can be penalised by the government).

An individual person is, generally speaking, a free thinking entity that goes about its business in a quiet and orderly fashion. *However,* when thrown together into a crowd the same individual can become unpredictable, illogical, reckless and violent. When drugs, alcohol and emotion are tossed into the mix, things can get out of hand. When this happens it is the police's job to restore order and normality, and where possible bring law breakers to justice.

Public order can be a challenging and occasionally (even the most fearless/macho officer would admit) a tad scary. Certain people have little regard for police officers at the best of times, so inevitably when enveloped in a riotous mob they will often only see a police uniform as a viable target for both verbal abuse and physical assault. They will have no consideration for the human being underneath the armour who is just doing their job and looking forward to going back home to their friends and family at the end of the shift. In the course of their regular duty, a hard-working police officer can expect to have their parentage questioned, their mother slandered, all manner of pork product related words sneered at them, as well as other abuse hurled in their direction; but in extreme public order scenarios it's bricks, bottles and petrol bombs that could be coming the officer's way as well.

FACT: During the riots of August 2011 throughout England, 186 police officers were injured. 5 members of the public lost their lives. 16,000 police officers from forces all over the country were deployed in London alone to restore order. An estimated £200 million worth of property was damaged. Approximately 3,500 people were arrested as a result.

I Predict a Riot

When an officer has sufficient experience they may apply to undertake specialist 'riot' training to be a police support unit (or PSU) officer. PSU training in the United Kingdom is voluntary tactical training undertaken by selected candidates that provides those officers with the skills required to safely and effectively deal with a variety of public order situations outside the remit or capability of regular divisional officers. The initial basic training consists of a 4- to 5-day course at one of several specialist training facilities located up and down the country. A PSU officer will generally undertake their normal duties until such time that they are called upon to perform this specialist role at either a pre-planned operation or when disorder erupts and the brown stuff hits the fan.

There are 3 grades of PSU officer:

> *Level 3* – The very basic training which all divisional officers receive. This simple training usually comes near the end of training school and involves foot duty cordons during which

officers generally wear their standard-issue uniform – e.g. high-visibility jackets under stab vests, custodian helmets for men and bowler hats for women. To attain this level, officers must demonstrate they know their left from their right (this catches a few out), have the ability to walk in a straight line whilst in formation (this catches a lot out), form simple cordons that none shall pass whilst saying "nothing to see her, move along", and very occasionally shout loudly at would-be rioters whilst waving their batons around menacingly.

Level 2 – This is the standard PSU level which officers attain when taking their initial PSU course. Standard kit for PSU officers consists of a transparent acrylic riot shield, a baton, a visored 'NATO' helmet, shin, shoulder and elbow guards, along with fireproof coveralls and the very important groin protector. Until recently, level 2 officers had to be able to run 500 metres dressed in full protective equipment whilst carrying a long shield (clear Perspex shield approximately 1.5 metres tall) in less than 2 mins 45 secs. This was a reasonably challenging feat; however it has now been replaced with the much more easily attainable level 6.3 on the bleep test mentioned previously, wearing any gym kit and not carrying anything (the Metropolitan Police of London still use the 500m shield run).

Level 1 – The rarest of all PSU officers, they receive regular training which can be every five weeks. Their specialist training is in shield tactics, violent persons, petrol bombing, as well as house entry and search. They are usually employed full time in their PSU role and only found in larger, city forces. All public order officers need to be fit, but a level 1 officer must be able to run 1000 metres, dressed in full protective equipment whilst carrying a long shield, in less than 6 minutes. This is no mean feat when considering the officer is encumbered by kit and shield weighing 25 – 35 kg.

In reality, PSU real life commitments generally involve officers waiting around in a van for several hours in full protective kit with all the other officers, talking rubbish, spreading the latest station gossip, and trying to work out who has the best flatulence. For most, the public order training – the initial course and subsequent refreshers – is a welcome distraction and fantastic fun which gives officers a chance to at least leave the van and practise their skills.

The training facilities are designed to replicate shopping precincts and housing estates so that officers can practice negotiating the area whilst working as part of a team called a 'serial', which in turn forms a bigger team referred to as a police support unit (or PSU). A single PSU consists of three serials, each in a police van (or carrier). Each serial/van will contain a sergeant, six constables and a designated van driver. Overseeing all three vans and completing the PSU will be an officer of 'Inspector' rank. A PSU may also be supported by specialist trained 'medics' (first aid specialists to treat officers, members of the public *and* rioters), 'evidence gatherers' (officers whose purpose it is to record the crowd with video cameras with the intention of later prosecuting any identifiable offenders) and 'field intelligence team' (FIT) – officers who overtly attempt to engage with the crowd, especially the ring leaders, with the hope of gathering intelligence and ultimately negotiating a peaceful conclusion.

During serious civil unrest, police forces may require dozens (or even more) PSUs to tame their unruly population. In these instances, when unable to muster enough officers of their own, the local force relies on neighbouring forces to provide reinforcements so all officers are trained in the same tactics nationally. This assistance is referred to as 'mutual aid' and was seen on a huge scale in the summer riots of August 2011 where officers from all over the country worked around the clock to assist their colleagues.

PSU tactics are based around use of shields and strategic formations designed to control crowds and to either advance into, hold onto, or (occasionally) tactically withdraw from territories, in order to protect property and people. During their training, having practiced the tactics, officers will be thrown into as real life as possible scenarios with specific objectives outlined at the outset. During the scenarios, crowds will hurl abuse and missiles at the officers, as well as the occasional petrol bomb. When still training but not performing the role of PSU officers, police officers get the chance to form the riotous mob and to hurl projectiles and colourful language at their colleagues – strictly for their training benefit of course. If your arm is good enough you might even get to bounce a lump of wood off a supervisor's head! Sergeants normally stand behind the row of their constables so you will have to have a good arm to land a missile plumb on their helmet; if you are a thrower of Olympic standard you might even land one on the Inspector right at the back of the PSU! There are not many jobs in the world where you get the chance to lawfully throw bricks at your supervisor's faces in the interests of their personal development, so constables do not like to miss the opportunity and usually seize it with gusto!

Like most policing in the UK, the media spotlight is constantly focused on the behaviour of officers – both individually and collectively – during public order situations. As such, police tactics are constantly evolving to fit public opinion. Presently a softer, more engaging strategy is favoured during disorders with the intention of capturing video evidence of offenders (via CCTV and the evidence gathering officers) committing crime so that they can be later identified and arrested, rather than risk inflaming a situation further by arresting them there and then during the disorder. Getting the balance between robust and effective policing, whilst still allowing people the freedom to voice their views whilst not infringing their human rights, is a tricky one.

*POWER: Section 60 of the Criminal Justice and Public Order Act 1994 gives police the power to search **any** person found in a defined geographical area, within a set time period, without the necessity for the grounds normally required for 'Stop & Search'. When in effect the same section also outlaws the wearing of face masks or disguises. This tactical option has to be authorized by a senior officer and is used to tackle football hooliganism, gang fights or expected large civil disorders.*

Drunk and Disorderly

Fortunately full scale riots are rare and not all public order situations involve officers dressing up like Power Rangers and having to fend off a blood-thirsty mob. Basic public order policing happens every weekend when people hit the streets to spend their hard-earned wages (or benefit money) at licensed premises. The police refer to this as 'night time economy' public order.

Drunk people are the bane of a police officer's life I can assure you.

Have you ever been to a party and you're the only sober person there and you feel slightly uncomfortable as you don't know anyone else? It's a slightly unsettling atmosphere and time is dragging as you look at your watch for the seventh time since arriving. In fact you're not really sure why you've been invited or agreed to go in the first place and now people keep staring at you. You knew the party host from school but if honest, you haven't properly kept in contact and their new friends just seem weird and childish. It's awkward and really you just want to be at home watching *Match Of The Day* or a show presented by that delightful Ant and Dec. Any of this sound familiar? Well that's the feeling every police officer has, standing outside licensed venues at the weekend.

As I once again find myself on public order duty on Saturday night, standing outside Lava and Lights night club – waiting for the inevitable fight to happen in front of me, whilst at the same time attempting to reassure the public they are safe – I see him. Him being the drunk male with the gormless smile across his sweaty face. He'll wander around outside the club with the smokers who are busy chatting and swearing away at each other. It is obvious he has no mates of his own, no money left, but although it's 3:45 a.m. in the morning, he also has no intention of ending the evening until everyone has got in taxis and the streets are awash with Subway wrappers and bodily fluids. I watch as he bumbles around, desperately trying to find someone to talk to and show interest and/or take pity on him. My 'scroat-dar' is going haywire.

But then I make the ultimate mistake! I've made eye contact with him! I see his grin swell and his eyes cross as he tries to focus on me before he begins to stumble in my general direction.

"Oh no, please leave me alone," I mutter to myself as he approaches.

But just as the youth is about to open his mouth and utter something enlightening, I am afforded a brief respite: a little blonde, barely wearing a skirt and top despite the near sub-zero temperature, projectile-vomits just a few feet away from me. The crowd turns to look at the young girl and cheers before returning to their socializing. My 'buddy' PC Knightly (officers always stay in pairs on public order duty) goes over to see if she is OK ... and gets a second burst of sick over her boots for her trouble.

"She is well fit," slurs the male youth at the puking blonde before turning his attention back to me as he remembers why he started the intoxicated and therefore perilous journey across the pavement.

He is just a few feet away now and only a miracle can save me from having to interact with him. I know what's coming so with a deep sigh I prepare for the witty banter that's bound to shortly spew forth from his noise hole.

But suddenly, as he makes his final approach, a feeling of personal disappointment comes over me: maybe, despite my months of training and years of experience, I prejudged the youth and he has a serious legal question to ask and needs my assistance. A distant memory about why I signed up for this job in the first place comes back to the forefront of my mind – to help the public! As a protector of the Queen's peace and public servant, I have a responsibility – nay, duty – to aid this inebriated citizen. I straighten up, puff out my chest, turn my ear to him, and wait to hear what the tanked-up gentleman has to say...

"If a woman's pregnant, yeah, do you have to let

her p*ss in your hat?"

My heart sinks and a little piece of me dies inside. I should have trusted my first instinct. I tell the male to clear off before I lock him up for the night for a public order offence. He wisely heeds my advice and once again shuffles off into the crowd to find someone else whose evening he can enhance as he has done mine. I used to at least try to engage revellers and make polite conversation when I was new. Now I just manage to resist the temptation to hand out Section 5 warnings to anyone who dares come within 5 metres of my proximity.

PS. By the way, no woman, pregnant or otherwise, has ever urinated in my hat either with or without my consent. Another police myth dispelled.

PPS. A Section 5 warning refers to Section 5 of The Public Order Act 1986: when a person, who is in a public place, behaves in such a way that another person within the hearing or sight of that person is likely to be caused harassment, alarm or distress, a Section 5 Public Order offence has been committed. This is the lowest level of offence under this Act; however it is also the most commonly committed and subsequently facilitates many arrests.

POWER: Section 50 of the Police Reform Act 2002 states the police have the power to demand the name and address of anyone they reasonable believe to be engaged in anti-social behaviour.

Top 10 Things Drunk People Say to the Police:

As well as asking about the legal rights of expectant

women using police headwear as potties, inebriated party people jump at the opportunity to babble on to the men and women in blue about all manner of nonsense at the weekends. The officers are actually there to protect the nation's high streets and nightspots and *not* provide entertainment for club-goers. In fairness not every boozed up person is a menace; from time to time, whilst on duty it is possible to have insightful and intelligent debate with people on a night out which makes the shift pass quicker as well as helping portray the police in a friendly and approachable light. This is often not the case though.

1. *"Do you know my best mate Steve? He's a copper."*

Despite only knowing their good friend's first name, members of the public expect a police officer to know every other police officer in the country – irrespective of whether Steve even works for the same force as them. No, I do not know Steve.

2. *"I fancy a bacon sandwich."*

The old ones are not necessarily the best ones. This one is slurred with a broad smile across their face and usually precedes a public order warning being issued by the less-than-amused officer. A very predictable and disappointing effort from the boozed up amateur comedian.

3. *"I didn't do it! Ha ha!"*

Comedy gold. The drunken and over-excitable person will humorously insinuate that the officer standing outside the pub or club is there to arrest them. Sometimes there is a little variant on this classic when they laugh and shout "OK, you got me, I did it!" offering out their hands to be arrested. One day I might just call their bluff by deliberately misinterpreting their poor attempt at humour and take their joking as a genuine confession and slap the cuffs on them, thus improving my arrest figures and clearing some of my crime reports.

4. "It took 18 officers to arrest me last time!"

This is a lie; with budget cutbacks, most police forces couldn't muster 18 officers being in one place at the same time without a meticulously, pre-planned operation being in effect. Undesirables take great pride in gloating about how so many officers were present in order to arrest them last time. The truth is that the more officers there are to arrest a subject, then the less likely that person is going to be subjected to injury. Officers train to work as a team to restrain villains with as minimal an amount of force being exerted as necessary.

5. "Will you give me a lift home please, I've lost all my money?"

No. 999 Taxis only drop off at one location – the rooms are free but sparsely furnished with no minibar. Usually when they say 'lost' they actually mean 'spent' their money on copious amounts of alcoholic beverages.

6. "You wouldn't be saying that if you weren't in uniform!"

Possibly not, because then I would be some weirdo vigilante out bossing about members of the public. But since I am wearing the uniform, and someone has to keep the peace, I will tell those that need telling to behave or suffer the consequences.

7. *"Have you found my bike yet? It got nicked ages ago and you lot have done nothing!"*

I didn't even know I was supposed to be looking! I've never met you before or know anything about your stolen bike. I'm very sorry we have failed you thus far, but I'll now drop everything and make it my top priority! I sympathise with victims of crime and wherever possible my colleagues and I will do our utmost to reunite them with their property, but sometimes it is just not possible.

8. *"Why don't you go and catch real criminals?"*

Because we're too busy dealing with drunken idiots right now.

9. *"That doorman has just assaulted me! I want him arrested!"*

It is true that some door staff are overly heavy-handed and when they cross that line they should still be dealt with by the law; but if the police arrested every security officer following a boozy complaint from a recently ejected customer, then soon no venues across the country would be able to open. Actually, that doesn't sound such a bad idea...

10. *"You're right officer: I've had a lovely evening, but as you suggest I'm going to go home now before I do something silly and spoil it all as a result of my intoxication. Keep up the good work. Cheerio!"*

NB. *One of the ten above I made up and has never been said to a police officer ever before. Can you guess which one?*

18. Best of the Rest

Finally I will tell you about some of the more pertinent and/or most common incidents that front-line officers attend, but that didn't warrant a chapter of their own.

Abandoned 999 – *very common*

These are a very regular occurrence. If an emergency call is made but either there is no response at all from the caller, or only part of a message is passed to the call taker, then police assume the worst and an officer is dispatched. The telephone numbers emergency calls come in on are all recorded (as are the content of the calls themselves) and from 'subscriber checks' from the respective phone companies – mobile and landlines – police can find out the address associated with that particular number. Often these types of jobs are graded for a quick response just in case, so it is usually time for the officer to fire up the blues & twos and get a move on!

    Waiting at the other end of the phone line for an officer can be anything from a confused parent holding an inquisitive toddler who has gotten hold of the phone, to a full scale domestic bloodbath, or anywhere in between.

Animals in the Road – *fairly common in rural locations, less so in inner-city areas*

This is a great example of a job that falls by default into

the police remit as it doesn't fall into anyone else's. I occasionally find myself minding my own business, out patrolling in the country, when I'm called to a 'Highway Obstruction'. Usually, after several minutes of searching, as the helpful member of the public cannot describe their exact location other than that they're "by a big tree, next to a stone wall", I find myself presented with a small herd of animals recently escaped from a farmer's field.

The trouble with horses, cows, sheep et al is that they won't listen to reason: no matter how much you implore them to move, they stubbornly remain. Surprisingly no instruction in horse-whispering, rodeo-riding or anything else that might be helpful in this situation is given at training school.

Police do have something called the National Decision Making Model' (previously called the 'Conflict Management Model') to help deal with belligerent humans, but to my cost I have found this is futile on anything with four legs. Please allow me to demonstrate:

PC Surname: *"Please can you move?"*
Cow: *"Moo."*
PC Surname: *"You're holding up traffic and impacting on innocent motorists' lives."* [MOPs helpfully illustrate the point by sounding their horns behind me as they grow impatient.]
Cow: *"Moo."*
PC Surname: *"Think of your family, Daisy, what would they say if they could see you now?"*
Cow: *"Moo."*
PC Surname: *"Oh, please move, I don't need this right now, I've got crime reports to update."*

Cow: *"Moo."*
PC Surname: *"I must insist you move NOW, obstructing the highway is an arrestable offence."*
Cow: [No response, begins to defecate in the road.]
PC Surname: *"Is there anything I can reasonably say or do to get you to mooove?"* [Get it?]
Cow: *"Moo."*
PC Surname: *"Right! Move now or I will use force!"* [Baton drawn.]
Cow: *"Moooo!"* [Cow charges at PC Surname who turns and flees, screaming like a child.]
You get the picture...

Snow Days – *mostly only during winter*

When even the lightest covering of snow kisses the ground, this grand country of ours, which once had the greatest empire in the world, now grinds to a halt. Whilst severe weather warnings advise MOPs to stay at home and watch Phillip and Holly on *This Morning* and only to venture out when absolutely necessary, emergency service workers are told to get their butts to work by hook or by crook.

Despite the chaos, snow days can be fun: blue-light runs take on a whole new scary and challenging dimension, burglary rates fall considerably as everyone is at home to guard their things, and (other than RTCs) officers spend most of their time chasing away naughty children who are pelting houses with snowballs.

Smithy and I once tried to start a playful snowball fight with the children from the Chavington Manor estate, but it had to be abandoned half way through when one of the Butcher spawns threw the first petrol bomb.

TOPTIP: Do not allow colleagues to film you using riot shields as makeshift sledges before uploading it to YouTube.

FACT: Snowball-related violence increases exponentially during the months of December to February compared to the months of June through to August!

Special Holidays – *fairly consistent (although New Year's Eve somehow still seems to take Duty Planning by surprise every time as they never roster enough officers to work!)*

Christmas, New Year, Bonfire Night, Halloween, any Bank Holiday weekends: all joyous occasions to be celebrated – unless you happen to be a police officer working at the time (particularly at night). Policing those particular drunken evenings soon sucks out any frivolity these previously special childhood events once held – if you have ever been witness to Jack Sparrow being brutally assaulted by Spiderman as Wonder Woman and the Blues Brothers look on during a cold October evening, you will know what I mean.

MOWP/Bilking – *very common*

Due to spiralling fuel prices, making off without payment (MOWP), or 'bilking' to give it its 'ye olde' legal name, is now a regular pastime for certain members of the criminal class. Most are not stupid enough to attempt this with their own number plates displayed, so stolen plates are the order of the day (see 'theft from motor vehicles' below).

Forces have 'Forecourt Crime' departments who exclusively deal with fuel thefts and attempt to identify the offenders from the available CCTV.

Should such a theft occur (and if the usually spotty teenager working at the petrol station is perceptive enough to call the police) a vehicle description along with registration number will be passed over the police radio for all units in the area to pay passing attention. Should an officer be lucky enough to find the vehicle a quick and easy arrest usually follows; or – if the officer is really lucky – maybe even a pursuit!

Neighbour Disputes – *common*

Some people just cannot get on with anyone. Not being content with getting a free house from the council, some families even like to choose who they live next door to. If they do not like the pairing that the council has given them, a neighbour feud commences which the police must referee. Hostilities usually start with a bit of traditional name-calling over the fence, but quickly escalate to missiles being thrown, cars being damaged, accusations and counter-accusations, before moving on to full-scale conflicts of the like seen in fair Verona, where civil blood makes civil hands unclean, etc.

Some forces still have neighbourhood teams who try to nip any unpleasantries in the bud before they get out of hand. Unfortunately, due to government cuts, there are increasingly fewer neighbourhood officers as resources are diverted to priority front-line policing.

The challenge with this type of job is not to take sides, but instead to mediate between the two warring factions as best as possible, whilst dealing with any specific criminal matters that present themselves. In some cases both bickering families are equally horrible – as demonstrated by their failure to behave like sensible, civil human beings towards each other – so the officer now embroiled in the dispute will dislike both equally, thus making side-taking not an issue.

In these situations it is important the police involve 'partner agencies' like local councils and housing associations who can take equal ownership of the problem and either pacify both, or move on one of the parties involved so that they can start aggravating a new community elsewhere. (Preferably in a new police division or, better still, a whole new police force area.)

Break-in in Progress/ Intruder Alarm – *common (but not common enough)*

Catching a burglar halfway out of a window with a flat-screen TV in his grubby little hands is the holy grail for police officers. Burglars are the lowest of the low and cause untold misery to their usually distraught victim.

Nothing gets an officer more excited than the report of a potential break-in in progress that usually originates from a neighbour or alarm company. When this happens, it's time to bring the noise and drive the wheels off the panda to get to the scene – always in a controlled and safe fashion of course.

Very occasionally, officers arrive in time and the despicable intruder is arrested. More frequently it turns out to be the homeowners' absent-minded son climbing through the window as he has forgotten his key; other times the unsuspecting cleaner who has forgotten the alarm code gets the fright of their life when several enthusiastic and over-excitable police officers come bowling through the door, tripping over Henry the Hoover as they do so, before pouncing on them over-zealously.

Hospital Transport – *very common*

There is a medical condition that is highly infectious, has varying symptoms, but fortunately no long-term consequences. The condition is 'Custoditus'. Thousands of prisoners a year are struck down by the illness immediately upon entering a police station – or certainly within a few hours of boredom spent inside an 8'-by-10' cell.

The illness usually manifests itself in chest pains, dizziness, stomach cramps and any other symptom that cannot be proved or disproved by a contracted health care professional (HCP) in police custody. In the most extreme cases, budding thespians have even been known to fit, convulse or faint – but only when they know an officer or CCTV is watching.

Because the death of a prisoner in police contact (whilst in a police station or for up to 24 hours after being released) can reflect badly on a custody sergeant's future promotion hopes (not to mention ongoing employment and pension), if there is even the remotest chance a prisoner may be genuinely ill, an ambulance will be called and the handcuffed prisoner will be whisked off to a hospital waiting room which is of course much more entertaining than the cell.

Sadly, asking the prisoner to pop back to the nick once they have been confirmed faking is usually a forlorn exercise. So that means two highly trained, fully equipped, undoubtedly overloaded, and moderately paid police officers must accompany the villain to the accident and emergency department and wait with them to be seen.

But do not despair; there is a respite for the poor officers stuck for hours in the waiting area: the 'Guess the Injury Game'! Very simple to play so I'm sure I do not need to explain. Now I'm not saying that the game is so enjoyable it is worth a trip down the hospital on your day off, but if you're there already you might as well make the most of it.

Suspicious Packages – *rare*

Unattended packages can be one of three things: there is a minute possibility it could be a bomb; an even more minuscule chance it could be a toxic white powder such as anthrax; most likely it will be someone's packed lunch or luggage that they left behind by accident. We don't call them 'bombs' as those are black spheres with a rope-like fuse coming out the top and are only seen in cartoons; instead we call them improvised explosive devices (IEDs). If this all sounds a bit military, then it's because it is: the police training comes straight out of an MOD manual.

In the event of a member of the public finding a package likely to be an explosive, police cordons are immediately placed around it and the area cleared of civilians. A lone first responder (preferably a probationary constable as less time, effort and expense has been invested in their training to that point) will be sent forward to have a good look at the package. With their radio and mobile phone switched off (so that no signal can accidentally detonate the device) the officer will have a good gander at what he/she can see and maybe even doodle a little sketch of it in their PNB. This will all be fed back to the gold commander (a senior ranking officer who will take charge in 'critical incidents' such as this) and the army 'explosive ordnance device' (EOD) team will be called out (think *The Hurt Locker* but far less over-dramatic and American). The army will turn up and send a *Short-Circuit*-Johnny-5-style robot out to examine the package and most likely fire a large metal disrupting bolt at the device to disable it, or blow it into a million pieces – sending cheese and pickle sandwiches and a Capri Sun (or alternatively underwear and socks) everywhere as it turns out it was a packed lunch or luggage. It is rare that the army have to get up close and personal for 'red wire or blue wire?' dilemmas.

If it is a suspected toxic powder, much the same happens, however the police officer inspecting the package will be a specially trained 'chemical, biological, radioactive or nuclear' (CBRN) officer. For their protection, they will be sporting a military airtight suit similar to the ones scientists wear in zombie movies to shield them from the airborne virus (only in the film, one suit always rips and the scientist then tries to eat his colleagues' brains before one of his former best friends is forced to execute him in a highly emotional scene).

Whilst still on the subject, rather amusingly every so often an MOP brings into the station something like an unexploded WW2 grenade that they found when clearing out their granddad's house. At this point the grenade is immediately placed on the floor in the police station enquiry office, chaos ensues and the whole building is evacuated so the army can pop along to do their thing again! After several hours of disruption the army determines it is a perfectly safe replica grenade and point out that in the Second World War the British army did not use hand grenades with 'Made in China' stamped on the bottom of them.

Sexual Offences – *fairly common*

Sexual offences range from a flasher in the park (the offence of 'outraging public decency'), to unwanted groping of one nightclub-goer by another ('sexual touching'), to the very worst kind which is of course rape. One thing is for sure: no officer likes these. A deathly silence usually follows a radio shout out for an officer to become available and volunteer to attend in the first instance a sexual-offences job. No takers means the radio controller will pick a police unit 'at random' to attend (only it's not always at random though – sometimes they pick the officer who offended them last week by being terse over the radio with them).

Sexual-offence jobs are unpleasant for everyone concerned, but especially the victim, which is what officers in attendance must remember, as becoming desensitized to a genuine victim's suffering can happen over time.

'Stranger rapes', i.e. those perpetrated on victims by an offender completely unknown to them, are fortunately rare. Most involve current or ex-partners, over-amorous friends or recent acquaintances. Often alcohol and/or drugs are an aggravating factor too.

Resource permitting, once a response unit has spoken with the victim, a specially trained officer will take over and gain an account from them. Forces will have an investigation unit specifically tasked to deal with sexual offences; however they tend to be a Monday to Friday, 9 a.m. to 5 p.m. type setup and it is very rare for a rape to occur on a Tuesday morning for example. Instead, they usually get reported at night – near the end of an officer's shift – meaning that officer will inevitably be getting off late again as it's insensitive to tell a tearful, gushing victim to wind up her story mid-flow as you're off in half an hour.

A front-line officer who has volunteered for the specialist training will be plucked from Division. Usually the victim can give a description of the suspect – if not name them and tell the police where they live – however, as there tend not to be independent witnesses and therefore, without corroborative evidence, it's one word against another, once again forensics are the best weapon in the police arsenal for a successful prosecution.

The clothes worn by the victim at the time of the offence will be seized along with a urine sample of theirs. Any identifiable crime scene will be examined and again items seized (such as bed sheets). Finally the victim will be asked to undergo a medical examination by a qualified doctor that can also tell if intercourse has taken place and the people involved. In honesty, the whole process is uncomfortable and intrusive for the victim, despite as much discretion being employed as possible.

FACT: Accurate statistics regarding this 'taboo' subject are sparse, but the 2006/07 British Crime Survey interviewed women aged 16 to 59 in England and Wales and found 0.5% (1 in every 200) reported that they had suffered rape or attempted rape in the previous year, equating to approximately 85,000 nationally. That same year, less than 800 persons were convicted of rape. Of course not all sexual offence victims are female. Prevention, education and convictions are improving but there is still much to do.

Once in custody, the suspect will be placed in a 'dry cell' (one without access to water to prevent them washing away evidence) and be invited – there is no power to take by force – to provide forensic samples if the time scale between the offence and then allows. This could be hand swabs, fingernail scrapings or even penal swabs. (Do not fear, the latter is done by a qualified doctor, not the new PC on shift!) Although the accused can refuse to give samples, they will have to account for why in interview and proper inference can be drawn.

Criminal Damage – *very common*

This is when a person deliberately causes damage to property belonging to another, or behaves recklessly and as a result causes damage (even if it wasn't their intention). A criminal damage varies from petty vandalism, to spiteful damage caused by ex-partners or disgruntled neighbours, up to large scale arsons that cause untold financial damage. The 'victim' might be a person or an organisation (such as the local council). In the case of lower-level crimes (the ones front-line officers deal with) it is all about witnesses – did anyone see it happen or was it captured on CCTV? If not, it will be hard to secure a prosecution without an admission from someone, and often all the officer will be able to offer is sympathy and a crime number for the injured party's insurance company claim.

If there is sufficient evidence to identify and prosecute the offender, compensation for the damage could be paid via a conditional caution or an award via the courts to the victim. (The only problem is that this is sometimes direct from the offender's benefits at just £2 a week for the rest of their lives!)

Sporting Events/Concerts – *variable*

If you're lucky enough to have a major sports team or venue in your region then you can expect to have your weekends disrupted with work on a regular basis. Depending on how kind your force is – as well as how their overtime budget is looking – this may be optional paid overtime, or alternatively working may be forced upon you.

If you happen to have a fondness for the local team anyway, do not be fooled into thinking that this means free entry and a front-row seat; sadly even if you make it into the stadium and pitch side, most of your time is spent with your back to the entertainment as you scan the crowd for signs of trouble.

You will however get to have a bit of friendly banter with paying punters: my personal favourite is when 5,000 football fans tunefully chant at me, "Who's that tw*t with a nipple on his hat" referring to the male custodian headdress that, in truth, is rather breast shaped. I've even found myself humming the catchy tune on the way home from work a couple of times.

Often there will be a PSU contingent outside sports grounds, especially when rival or national teams are competing as some young men (and quite a few middle aged ones too) just can't help themselves. Thankfully the English national football team do their bit to help the already strained police service by regularly getting knocked out of competitions very early on.

Assaults – *ridiculously common*

Having had the good sense to pick up this publication I will not insult you by explaining what an assault entails as I am sure you already know. I will however explain the different grades of assault as many people ask. Although still open to interpretation, the Crown Prosecution Service summarises as follows (in ascending seriousness):

Common Assault
- *Grazes*
- *Scratches*
- *Abrasions*

- *Minor bruising*
- *Swelling*
- *Reddening of the skin*
- *Superficial cuts*
- *'Black eyes'*

Section 47 Assault or Actual Bodily Harm (ABH)

- *Loss or breaking of teeth*
- *Temporary loss of sensory function, which may include loss of consciousness*
- *Extensive or multiple bruising*
- *Broken nose*
- *Minor fracture (to fingers, toes, etc.)*
- *Minor, but not merely superficial cuts requiring medical treatment (e.g. stitches or gluing)*
- *Psychiatric injury that is more than mere emotions such as fear, panic or distress*

Section 20 Wounding Grievous Bodily Harm (GBH)

- *Injury resulting in permanent disability or permanent loss of sensory function*
- *Injury resulting in more than minor permanent, visible disfigurement; broken or displaced bones/limbs, including fractured skull*
- *Compound fractures such as broken cheek bones, jaw, ribs, etc.*
- *Injuries which cause substantial loss of blood, usually necessitating a transfusion*
- *Injuries resulting in lengthy treatment or incapacity*
- *Extreme psychiatric injury*

Section 18 Wounding with Intent (GHB with Intent)

- *Injuries as above however more serious an offence as the offender showed the deliberate intention to cause the injuries.*

TOMV, TWOC, TFMV – *very common*

The above abbreviations won't score you any points in Scrabble, but instead relate to vehicle crime. Offences like this are termed 'volume crime' because they occur regularly and will be dealt with by either front-line police officers and/or the basic investigation teams.

To clarify, theft of motor vehicle (TOMV) occurs when a car is stolen and not returned at all or, when it is found, it is then in an unusable state e.g. left burnt-out on the outskirts of a traveller site. If you were paying attention earlier you will recall in order for a theft of something to have occurred, the thief has to have the intention to permanently deprive the owner of it. If the vehicle is stolen, but subsequently recovered, and it cannot be proved the intention was to permanently deprive, then we have a TWOC (taken without owner's consent). This might include domestic TWOCs where a partner or offspring takes a vehicle without checking with their furious family member. If a vehicle is damaged whilst in a state of TWOC then it is called an 'aggravated TWOC' – not because Daddy is going to be even more livid with Junior though, it's just the legal term.

Finally there is theft from motor vehicle (TFMV) which is anything removed from or within a vehicle. Car radios have been replaced with mobile phones, laptops and SatNavs as the preferred targets in these instances. Number plates are also stolen, usually with the intention of fitting them to other cars to hide their true identity.

Sympathetic/Death Message- rare

Although never pleasant (but not as hard as many civilian folk might think) 'passing a sympathetic' involves calling in person at an address and explaining to the occupant that a friend or family member is either injured and in hospital, or has passed away.

Although very little (if any) training is given to new officers about how to pass on this difficult information, most experienced officers would recommend an empathetic but direct and straight-to-the-point approach. Reactions by the receiver can be mixed – some will seem unperplexed and not bothered, others will cry hysterically; occasionally they have been known to lose all control and lash out at the messenger.

Wearing the uniform sometimes acts as a shield, protecting the officer from the personal impact and unpleasantness of certain tasks.

19. FAQs

I've already answered the question about pregnant women and officers' hats. But if, despite reading this book, you're for some reason still harbouring a slightly warm (albeit no longer burning) desire and ambition to one day enroll in the police ranks, below are some of the more frequently asked questions by curious members of the public.

Is being a police officer dangerous?

Potentially yes, as even if you follow your training, take the time to dynamically risk-assess every situation presented, and don't take any gung-ho gambles, there are still a lot of unpredictable, violent lunatics out there. If it is comforting to know, serious injuries to officers are rare and in reality the odd bit of danger, intrigue and unexpectedness is what appeals to many in the job and makes it like no other.

Do I have to work night shifts?

Certainly for the early years you will. Once experienced, there are roles with hours more socially and family orientated. Often recruits are surprised how quickly they adapt to the hours, but if the prospect of shift work really does not appeal, maybe it is best to look elsewhere.

From 2012, following the government's Winsor Report into police pay and practices, police shift workers on duty during unsociable hours receive additional earnings for their efforts.

Is there lots of paperwork?

Yes, have you not been paying attention?

Can I have a day off?

Like an insomniac on Red Bull, crime never sleeps! A good copper is never off duty! But more seriously: maybe, if you're very lucky. Officers are entitled to 22 days annual leave on employment commencement, rising to 25 days after two years' service. This continues to increase up to 30 days a year when an officer reaches 20 years' service.

Bear in mind that officers can be (and regularly are) refused leave applications, *and* can also be directed to work at very short notice on rest days. If instructed to work on a day off (this may be because of a shortage of resources, special operations, court appearances, etc.) the officer will receive a 'rest day in lieu' (RDIL) that they can bank, to use at a later date (assuming the Duty Planning Department will allow them to take it on the day they want it!). As ever, do not underestimate the impact this incredible career will have on your personal life.

Will I be out on my own?

Each force will have their own policy towards crewing officers together; most will certainly pair officers together during the hours of darkness, but during the day resourcing usually dictates officers fly solo. Some sergeants will mix their units so that a few are single-crewed, whilst other cars are double-crewed 'incident response vehicles' or 'area cars' who can support each other at more potentially challenging/dangerous jobs. Police control room will not send an insufficient number of officers to a job likely to be highly dangerous.

Should I work near where I live?

Only you can answer that. There is no national policy stating an officer cannot live and work in the same area. If all your friends/family are criminals and likely to place you in compromising positions, maybe apply elsewhere.

I'm cocky and over-confident; can I go into Traffic, Firearms, or some other cool undercover unit straight away?

No.

Can I work part-time?

Yes you can. Many new mothers for example return to work part-time after maternity leave. However, for the training element at the beginning of a career, recruits are required to be available to work full-time hours. Speak with your local force's recruitment team who will be happy to assist.

Do you get to work out in the gym whilst on duty?

No, this is not the fire service! Some forces might have a pool/snooker or ping pong table if you're very lucky (not darts though – health and safety, don't you know), *but* if the Chief Inspector catches you then you'd better be able to come up with a good excuse as to why you are not out patrolling the streets and protecting the public.

Most forces have their own gym facilities which officers can use *off-duty* for free, as maintaining fitness is encouraged.

Do you get paid more in certain roles?

Generally speaking only rank affects pay; therefore a police constable on a response shift will earn the same as a detective constable, who will earn the same as a PC in the traffic department with the same amount of service, etc. Only when moving up the ranks will pay jump.

Veteran serving and retired officers tell me the job isn't the same now as it used to be and not to apply.

That's not actually a question. There is a famous and old saying amongst police folk: "The Job's f***ed!"

The same officers have been saying this for decades, but still they come to work. The job is changing and evolving constantly, but then it has to as so is the rest of the world. The current financial climate is placing the police service under great strain, but this is still an enjoyable and honourable profession.

I'm old. Can I still join?

Yes you can. There are some who receive the calling later in life and decide to embark on a change of career, or even second career. As long as you still have reasonable bladder control and are aged under 55 (upper age limit may vary for different forces) then welcome aboard. After all, experience is something that you cannot buy. There are also many 'mature' ex-military personnel in the police service so do not be put off.

20. Final Thoughts

So that is basically what a front-line police officer does, day in, day out, 365 days a year... only it isn't, as no two days are the same in this job and you can never know what awaits around the next street corner. In return for up to 35 years' loyal service, you can expect to see and do the most amazing things. To succeed takes commitment as it will literally change your life and outlook forever. This vocation is a lifestyle choice that will affect everything – but if you embrace it, a career in the police service can be a spectacular and rewarding choice.

I cannot apologise if this book seems cynical at times. This job is infinitely frustrating as the battle with crime and bureaucracy is a war that seems endless. There have been moments in my career when, out of frustration, I have thought about returning to the mundane but reliably predictable office job I had before. But when my head has cleared, I'm no longer a slave to the radio, and I'm finally off duty and thinking straight (usually with an alcoholic beverage in hand), I reflect and realise the trauma, strife and constant challenges are actually why I still love this job so much and could do nothing else.

I hope you have enjoyed the glimpse this book has given into police life and your interest and ambition has been enhanced. The job is not for everyone, but if you believe you could be one of the chosen few capable of dedicating your time so that others can benefit, I encourage you to make enquires with your local constabulary.

The police service is going through the greatest upheaval, overhaul and reform for 30 years. Admired by many countries, the British police are heralded as the greatest in the world; often imitated but never replicated. This is credit to the diligent, increasingly few front-line officers that continue to risk their lives daily so that unaware members of the public can go about their everyday lives in safety, and sleep soundly at night as police officers tirelessly patrol their streets.

Some love us, some despise us, but we perform our duties with pride and a steely determination in the knowledge that ours is the good fight. Why did we become police officers? Because we want to protect and stand up for those who cannot do so for themselves; because we care enough about the injustices in the world to do something about it. The British police will not be defeated in their ongoing battle against crime and disorder. We are a family. We are protectors of the Queen's peace. We are police officers. Come join us...

21. Glossary

There are huge amounts of jargon used in the police service. I cannot tell you them all here but, in keeping with the rest of this book, I can tell you some of the most commonly used terminology, abbreviations and slang. Some of the terms/phrases below you will have already come across throughout this book.

ABH – Actual Bodily Harm (assault)

ABE – abbreviation for Achieving Best Evidence. An ABE interview is one that is conducted in a specialist suite designed to appear more homely and welcoming, but still located within a police station. The interviewee will be asked questions by specially trained officers and all is video-recorded. ABE interviews are designed for particularly vulnerable victims or witnesses to make them feel at ease.

ACPO – Association of Chief Police Officers. A private limited company established in 1948 and made up by senior members of all England, Wales and Northern Ireland's police forces. ACPO coordinates national police operations, major investigations, cross-border policing and advises the government in matters such as terrorism and civil emergencies.

Affray – an offence under Section 3 of the Public Order Act 1986. Basically this amounts to fighting in the street (or any public place) whereby at least two protagonists are 'offenders'.

Airwave – radio digital communications system used by all police forces in the UK.

ANPR – abbreviation for Automatic Number Plate Recognition.

ASB – Anti-Social Behaviour. A blight on this country.

ASNT – abbreviation for 'Area Search, No Trace', meaning a police search of an area has been conducted but was negative.

Bash – police slang for a Road Traffic Collision.

Body snatcher – a most terrible sin. To body-snatch is to jump in and arrest someone who really should have been arrested by an officer who worked harder for the nick. Repeat offending makes officers very unpopular.

CBRN – abbreviation for chemical, biological, radiation and nuclear.

Centrex – Central Police Training and Development Authority.

CID – abbreviation for Criminal Investigation Department.

Common Law (Case Law) – Law not embodied in legislation. It consists of rules of law based on common custom and usage and on judicial (court) decisions.

CPS – Crown Prosecution Service. The government department responsible for prosecuting criminal cases investigated by the police in England and Wales.

CRO – Criminal Records Number.

Decamp – when suspects suddenly leave a vehicle on foot and attempt to flee their pursuers.

Eyeball – to have direct sight of a subject e.g. "I have 'eyeball' on the suspect's vehicle."

(The) Federation – Police officers aren't allowed to join a union, so they have a Federation instead. Also known as 'The Fed'.

Fishing – slang meaning the practice of actively going out and looking for drink drivers. Officers will pull over cars until they find a drunk driver.

FPN / Fixed Penalty Notice – one-off penalty issued to anti-social behaviour offenders for less serious offences than those that would warrant a Penalty Notice for Disorder (PND).

Garden hopping – to pursue an offender on foot over people's garden fences. Fantastic fun!

GBH – Grievous Bodily Harm (assault).

Hate Crime – any crime where the perpetrator's prejudice against an identifiable group of people is a factor in determining who is victimised. A victim of hate crime does not have to be from a minority or someone who is generally considered to be a 'vulnerable' person – anyone can be a victim of hate crime. Hate crime is one of the most under-reported crimes and a serious matter.

HATO – abbreviation for Highways Agency Transport Officer. HATO's assist the police with road disruptions.

HMCS – Her Majesty's Court Service.

HMIC – Her Majesty's Inspectorate of Constabulary. HMIC conducts inspections into the performance of every police force.

HORT1 (pronounced HORT-E) – form issued to a driver requiring him/her to produce driving documents in person at a nominated police station within 7 days. Commonly known as a 'producer'.

Incommunicado – In some cases it is necessary to deny prisoners in custody the right to have someone informed of their arrest. This is because evidence may be lost if word of their arrest is released. This is called placing a prisoner 'incommunicado' and can only be authorised by an officer of Inspector rank or above.

IP – Injured party / person or victim.

Livescan – automated system for scanning and recording fingerprints in custody units.

Making off – to try to get away from the police, usually on foot, e.g. "He's making off, control room! Send more units, over!"

Misper – a missing person.

M.O. – abbreviation for modus operandi.

MOP – member of public

MOPI – abbreviation for Management Of Police Information. Following an enquiry after the 2002 Soham murders, forces across England and Wales now use standardised systems to input and share information nationally.

NFA – abbreviation for 'No further action', or 'No fixed abode'.

NIM – National Intelligence Model. A standardised model for the management of information and intelligence.

NOK – next of kin.

Nominal – a person well known to police and likely to commit more crime.

NPIA – National Policing Improvement Agency.

PACE – The Police and Criminal Evidence Act (PACE) 1984. Significant piece of legislation providing the police with the powers they need to combat crime. PACE sets out to strike a balance between the powers of the police and the rights and freedoms of the public.

PCSO / Police Community Support Officers – provide a visible presence in the community, helping the police to tackle anti-social behaviour and offering reassurance to the public. They have strictly defined and limited powers which enable them to deal with specific crimes.

Phoenix Form – used to update the Police National Computer

(PNC) on crime activity such as custody details, bail conditions and Court results.

PNB – (Officer's) Pocket Notebook.

PNC – Police National Computer.

PND / Penalty Notice for Disorder – one-off penalty issued to anti-social behaviour offenders for more serious offences than a Fixed Penalty Notice (FPN).

PNLD – Police National Legal Database. An online legal information resource for officers to use. An invaluable research tool full of legal definitions, offence wordings and points to prove, with Home Office codes, as well as case law examples.

Point to Point or P2P – an Airwaves radio term meaning to privately call another officer or radio user without the rest of the radio channel hearing.

Polac or Polcol – a police traffic accident or collision. Damage caused to either the police car, another vehicle, or to a person's property (or in the worst case all three!).

Polsa – abbreviation for Police Search Advisor. An individual specially trained to assist and advise officers in strategic search techniques.

Potted – police slang meaning to be sent to prison, e.g. "I hear Wayne Butcher has been potted again for that assault."

Probie / Probationer – a student officer with less than two years' service.

Q – equals 'quiet'. A word never to be uttered mid-shift.

Refs – very rare occurrence: this is your food break.

Resume – to leave an incident and recommence patrol.

RIPA – (pronounced Ripper) Regulation of Investigatory Powers Act 2000. RIPA authority is required for surveillance to be conducted on a suspect.

RTC – abbreviation for 'Road Traffic Collision'. Previously known as an RTA or Road Traffic Accident, but amended as after all, not all crashes are accidents!

SB – Special Branch.

Scroat – slang. A member of the criminal underclass and those most likely to be of interest to the police.

SOCO/CSI – abbreviation for Scenes Of Crime Officer or Crime Scene Investigator; both are a civilian who specialises in forensic examination and investigation.

SOP – abbreviation for Standard Operating Procedure. Every type of police incident has a written SOP, which acts as a guide or aide memoire for dealing with such an incident.

Station cat – derogatory police slang for an officer who rarely, if ever, leaves the police station.

TFMV – Theft From Motor Vehicle.

Thief taker – police slang for an officer who has made a name for themselves with high arrest figures.

TIC / Taken into consideration – this is where, for example, a person is charged with a handful of burglaries and has admitted to committing several more, these additional crimes will be taken into consideration when sentence is passed.

TOMV – Theft Of Motor Vehicle.

Trumpton – slang, the second emergency service (fire brigade).

VAP – abbreviation for Violence Against the Person. Any offence where harm or threats are made to a human being (as opposed to property).

VIPER / Video Identification Parade Electronic Recording – this has replaced the traditional identity parade whereby the suspect and several others are lined up in a room for the hidden victim to view and identify (think Kevin Spacey and *The Usual Suspects*). It is now done via a monitor screen.

VODS / Vehicle Online Descriptive Search – a way of searching the 42 million records held on PNC to extract vehicles that match particular criteria, e.g. colour, model.

VRM – Vehicle Registration Mark.

Warrant card – a bit like an officer's badge. It will show the holder's name, rank, photo and warrant number (or collar number).

Dear Reader,

Amazon gives you the opportunity to rate and review this book whilst sharing your thoughts with friends and family on Facebook and Twitter. If you enjoyed this book and believe it is worth sharing, I would be forever grateful if you would take a few moments to leave an Amazon review on the website. I am a self-published author with a very small advertising budget and would appreciate your help so that I can continue to write about the police service.

Thank you very much and please check me out online:

www.facebook.com/pcsurname

www.pcsurname.blogspot.co.uk

Kind regards,

PC Surname

Want more from author PC Surname, Smithy, Knightly and the rest of the gang?

Law and Disorder: The Good, The Bad and The Police Officer

A follow up in paperback and electronic form will be available in 2013, see the Facebook page for more details!

Printed in Great Britain
by Amazon.co.uk, Ltd.,
Marston Gate.